Diana Yoshi

sushi
& sashimi

100 Great Recipes

APPLE

First published in the UK in 2012 by
Apple Press
7 Greenland Street
London NW1 0ND
United Kingdom
www.apple-press.com

This book was conceived, edited and designed by
McRae Publishing Ltd, London

NOTE TO OUR READERS

Eating eggs or egg whites that are not completely cooked poses the possibility
of salmonella food poisoning. The risk is greater for pregnant women, the elderly,
the very young, and persons with impaired immune systems. If you are concerned
about salmonella, you can use reconstituted powdered egg whites or pasteurized eggs.

Project Director Anne McRae
Art Director Marco Nardi

SUSHI & SASHIMI
Photography Brent Parker Jones
Text Diana Yoshi
Editing Christine Price, Daphne Trotter
Food Styling Lee Blaylock
Food Styling Assistant Rochelle Seator
Prop Styling Lee Blaylock
Layouts Aurora Granata
Prepress Filippo Delle Monache

ISBN 978-1-84543-486-1

Printed in China

contents

getting started

There are 100 tempting sushi recipes in this book. Many are simple and quick to prepare, while others require care and an eye for detail. They are all rated for difficulty: 1 (simple), 2 (fairly simple), or 3 (challenging). In these two pages we have highlighted 25 of the most enticing recipes, just to get you started!

GRILLED BELL PEPPER nigiri

TEX-MEX
sushi rolls

SALMON & CRAB
pressed sushi

VEGETARIAN
sushi balls

SALMON & TUNA
scattered sushi

TEMPURA SHRIMP
sushi rolls

STUFFED SQUID
sushi rolls

INSIDE-OUT
VEGETARIAN sushi rolls

SUSHI OMELET
money bags

RAINBOW sushi rolls

TOKYO-STYLE scattered sushi

CALIFORNIA sushi rolls

CLASSIC MACKEREL
pressed sushi

JAPANESE OMELET
nigiri

BATTLESHIP SUSHI
with teriyaki chicken

ROASTED VEGGIE
sushi rolls

NIGIRI platter

TUNA & VEGGIE
sushi cones

INSIDE-OUT CARROT & AVOCADO sushi rolls

RED SNAPPER
sashimi

BEST SUSHI ROLL

INSIDE-OUT OMELET
& AVOCADO sushi rolls

BEST NIGIRI

VEGETARIAN
sushi cones

BEST CONE SUSHI

SMOKED SALMON
& ASPARAGUS nigiri

BEST SASHIMI

SASHIMI
platter

BEST MISO SOUP

ENOKI MUSHROOM
& SCALLION miso soup

sushi rice

SUSHI rice

2¹/₂ cups (500 g) Japanese sushi rice (short-grain sticky rice)
3 cups (750 ml) water
¹/₄ cup (60 ml) Japanese rice wine vinegar
2 tablespoons sugar
1 teaspoon salt

Serves 4–8 • Preparation 10 minutes + 15 minutes to stand + about 1 hour to cool • Cooking 5 minutes • Difficulty 1

1. Wash the rice in a colander under cold running water until the water almost runs clear.

2. Place the rice and water in a medium saucepan, cover, and bring to a boil over medium heat. Reduce the heat to low and simmer for 5 minutes. Remove from the heat, cover, and let stand for 15 minutes.

3. Place the vinegar, sugar, and salt in a small saucepan and gently heat, stirring occasionally, until the sugar has dissolved. Remove from the heat and let cool.

4. Transfer the rice to a large bowl and stir in the vinegar mixture until well mixed. Set the rice aside until cool enough to handle. Use as indicated in the recipes.

If you liked this recipe, you will love these as well.

INSIDE-OUT SCALLOP & AVOCADO sushi rolls

JAPANESE OMELET nigiri

VEGETARIAN scattered sushi

sauces & garnishes

PICKLED ginger

8   ounces (250 g) fresh young ginger root
2   teaspoons salt
1   cup (250 ml) Japanese rice wine vinegar
$^1/_3$ cup (90 ml) water
4   tablespoons sugar

Makes about 2 cups (500 ml) • Preparation 15 minutes + 2–3 hours to rest + 5–7 days to pickle • Cooking 5 minutes • Difficulty 1

1. Wash the ginger carefully and scrub off the skin. Slice thinly with a sharp knife and place in a shallow bowl. Sprinkle with the salt and leave to rest for 2–3 hours.

2. Dry the slices of ginger with paper towels and place in a sterilized heat-resistant glass jar.

3. Mix the rice vinegar, water, and sugar in a small saucepan over medium heat, stirring until the sugar is dissolved. Bring to a boil then remove from the heat.

4. Pour the hot vinegar mixture into the jar over the ginger. Let cool and leave to pickle in the marinade, 5–7 days. As the ginger pickles it will turn a pale pink color. Keeps in the refrigerator for several weeks.

5. Allow about 2 tablespoons for each person when serving.

If you liked this recipe, you will love these as well.

STUFFED SQUID sushi rolls

INSIDE-OUT CARROT & AVOCADO sushi rolls

SMOKED SALMON & MANGO nigiri

CITRUS dipping sauce

Makes 1¼ cups (300 ml) • Preparation 5 minutes
Difficulty 1

½	cup (120 ml) soy sauce	½	cup (120 ml) freshly squeezed lemon juice
½	cup (120 ml) freshly squeezed grapefruit juice	¼	cup (60 ml) Japanese rice vinegar

1. Combine all the ingredients in a bowl and whisk until well mixed.

2. Pour into a bowl or jar, cover, and chill until required. Use as directed in the recipes. Keeps 2–3 days in the refrigerator.

SPICY mayonnaise

Makes 1¼ cups (300 ml) • Preparation 5 minutes
Difficulty 1

1	cup (250 ml) Japanese mayonnaise (or normal mayonnaise)
4	tablespoons (60 ml) Sriracha or other very spicy sweet chili sauce
1	teaspoon sesame oil

1. Put the mayonnaise in a small ceramic or glass bowl. Gradually stir in the Sriracha sauce and sesame oil, mixing until blended and pale pink.

2. Pour into a bowl or jar, cover, and chill until required. Keeps 2–3 days in the refrigerator.

3. Use the sauce as directed in the recipes, or in tuna or salmon sushi rolls, instead of wasabi. You can also serve it as a dipping sauce with other sushi dishes.

PICKLED cucumber garnish

Serves 4–8 • Preparation 15 minutes + 15 minutes to stand
Difficulty 1

1	small cucumber	½	teapoon sea salt
1	tablespoon rice wine vinegar	1	teapoon sugar

1. Slice the cucumber very thinly lengthwise into long strips.

2. Combine the cucumber strips in a bowl with the vinegar, salt, and sugar. Toss to coat and let stand for at least 15 minutes before draining.

3. Use the pickled cucumber strips to garnish all kinds of sushi dishes, from rolls to nigiri. Fold the strips of cucumber decoratively over or near the sushi.

SWEET chili sauce

Makes 2 cups (500 ml) • Preparation 30 minutes • Cooking 10 minutes • Difficulty 2

1	tablespoon peanut oil		spicy red chilis, very finely chopped
6	cloves garlic, finely chopped	1	tablespoon Thai fish sauce
2	shallots, finely chopped		
1	(14-ounce/400-g) can tomatoes, with juice	3	tablespoons Japanese rice wine vinegar
3½	ounces (100 g) very	3	tablespoons sugar

1. Heat the oil in a small saucepan over medium heat. Add the garlic and shallots and sauté until pale gold, 2–3 minutes.

2. Add the tomatoes and chilis. Bring to a boil then simmer over low heat. Stir in the fish sauce, vinegar, and sugar and simmer for 5 minutes. Remove from heat and allow to cool completely.

3. Transfer the sauce to a food processor and blend until most of the chili skins and seeds break down and the sauce is almost smooth.

4. Pour into a sterilized jar and refrigerate. Use within 5–7 days.

INSIDE-OUT OMELET & AVOCADO sushi rolls

1   recipe sushi rice (see page 7)

Omelet

4   large eggs
2   tablespoons sugar
1   teaspoon soy sauce
1   tablespoon butter

Sushi Rolls

5   nori sheets
2$\frac{1}{2}$ tablespoons spicy mayonnaise
     (see page 10)
1   avocado, peeled, pitted, and
     cut into long thin strips
4   ounces (120 g) orange flying
     fish roe

Serves 4–6 • Preparation 30 minutes + time for the rice • Cooking 10 minutes • Difficulty 2

1. Prepare the sushi rice.

Omelet

1. Crack the eggs into a bowl and whisk until smooth. Add the sugar and soy sauce, stirring until well mixed.

2. Heat a large frying pan over medium heat. Add the butter and tilt the pan to spread evenly over the bottom. Pour the egg mixture into the pan. When the egg is opaque and you can get a spatula under it without tearing, flip the omelet. When cooked through and pale golden brown, remove from the pan. Slice into $1\frac{1}{2}$ x $2\frac{1}{2}$-inch (4 x 6-cm) strips.

Sushi Rolls

1. Lay a nori sheet shiny side down on a clean work surface. Dip your hands in cold water to prevent the rice from sticking, and spread one-fifth of the rice evenly over the nori sheet, leaving a $\frac{1}{2}$-inch (1-cm) border on one long side.

2. Quickly turn the nori sheet over and place on a bamboo sushi mat. Spread $\frac{1}{2}$ tablespoon of mayonnaise over the nori. Lay strips of omelet and avocado lengthwise down the center of the nori sheet.

3. Use the sushi mat to firmly roll up to enclose the filling. Remove the mat and spread the sushi roll with a layer of fish roe using the back of the spoon. Turn the roll, coating as evenly as possible all over. Repeat with the remaining ingredients.

4. Place the rolls seam-side down on a chopping board. Trim the edges with a sharp knife and slice into rounds about 1 inch (2.5 cm) thick. Arrange on a platter and serve.

FRESH TUNA sushi rolls

1   recipe sushi rice (see page 7)
5   nori sheets
    Wasabi paste
8   ounces (250 g) sashimi-
    quality fresh tuna, cut into
    long thin strips
1   small cucumber, with peel,
    cut lengthwise into 5 strips
5   scallions (spring onions)
    Soy sauce, to serve
    Storebought or homemade
    pickled ginger (see page 9),
    to serve

Serves 4–6 • Preparation 30 minutes + time for the rice • Difficulty 2

1. Prepare the sushi rice.

2. Lay a nori sheet shiny side down on a bamboo sushi mat. Dip your hands in cold water to prevent the rice from sticking, and spread one-fifth of the rice evenly over the nori sheet, leaving a $1/2$-inch (1-cm) border on one long side.

3. Spread some wasabi lengthwise down the center of the rice. Lay strips of tuna, cucumber, and scallion over the wasabi. Lightly moisten the exposed nori edge with a little water. Using the sushi mat, firmly roll up to enclose the filling. Repeat with the remaining ingredients.

4. Place the rolls seam-side down on a chopping board. Trim the edges with a sharp knife and slice into rounds about 1 inch (2.5 cm) thick. Arrange on a platter and serve with the soy sauce and pickled ginger.

FRESH SALMON sushi rolls

1   recipe sushi rice (see page 7)
5   nori sheets
     Wasabi paste
7   ounces (200 g) sashimi-quality skinless fillet of fresh salmon, cut into $2^1/_2$ x $^1/_4$-inch (60 x 5-mm) batons
     Soy sauce, to serve
     Storebought or homemade pickled ginger (see page 9), to serve

Serves 4–6 • Preparation 30 minutes + time for the rice • Difficulty 2

1. Prepare the sushi rice.

2. Lay a nori sheet shiny side down on a bamboo sushi mat. Dip your hands in cold water to prevent the rice from sticking, and spread one-fifth of the rice evenly over the nori sheet, leaving a $^1/_2$-inch (1-cm) border on one long side.

3. Spread some wasabi lengthwise down the center of the rice. Lay strips of salmon over the wasabi. Lightly moisten the exposed nori edge with a little water. Using the sushi mat, firmly roll up to enclose the filling. Repeat with the remaining ingredients.

4. Place the rolls seam-side down on a chopping board. Trim the edges with a sharp knife and slice into rounds about 1 inch (2.5 cm) thick. Arrange on a platter and serve with the soy sauce, pickled ginger, and wasabi.

You will enjoy this "fusion" sushi roll recipe, which combines the exotic flavors of passionfruit with cream cheese and smoked salmon.

SALMON SUSHI ROLLS with passionfruit sauce

1   recipe sushi rice (see page 7)

Passion Fruit Sauce
3   passion fruit
$1/4$ cup (60 ml) vinegar
$1/4$ cup (50 g) sugar
1   clove garlic, finely chopped
     Salt

Sushi Rolls
1   avocado, peeled, pitted, and cut into $1/2$ inch (1 cm) strips
2   tablespoons freshly squeezed lemon juice
5   nori sheets
7   ounces (200 g) smoked salmon, cut into thin strips
1   mango, peeled, pitted and cut into $1/2$-inch (1-cm) strips
5   ounces (150 g) cream cheese, chilled until firm, cut into 2 x $1/4$-inch (50 x 5-mm) batons
     Black sesame seeds

Serves 4–6 • Preparation 30 minutes + time for the rice • Cooking 5 minutes • Difficulty 2

1. Prepare the sushi rice.

Passion Fruit Sauce

1. Cut the passionfruit in half and scrape the pulp into a bowl. Strain through a fine-mesh sieve, pressing with a spoon to extract all of the pulp and juice from the seeds. Discard the seeds and reserve the juice.

2. Combine the passionfruit juice, vinegar, sugar, and garlic in a saucepan and bring to a boil. Simmer until the sauce reduces and thickens, about 5 minutes. Remove from the heat and season with salt.

Sushi Rolls

1. Drizzle the avocado with the lemon juice. Lay a nori sheet shiny side down on a bamboo sushi mat. Dip your hands in cold water to prevent the rice from sticking, and spread one-fifth of the rice evenly over the nori sheet, leaving a $1/2$-inch (1-cm) border on one long side.

2. Lay strips of salmon, mango, and avocado lengthwise down the center of the rice. Top with some batons of cream cheese and drizzle with the passionfruit sauce. Sprinkle with the black sesame seeds. Lightly moisten the exposed nori edge with a little water. Using the sushi mat, firmly roll up to enclose the filling. Repeat with the remaining ingredients.

3. Place the rolls seam-side down on a chopping board. Trim the edges with a sharp knife and slice into rounds about 1 inch (2.5 cm) thick. Arrange on a platter and serve.

TERIYAKI BEEF sushi rolls

Teriyaki Beef

$1/4$	cup (60 ml) soy sauce
$1/4$	cup (60 ml) mirin
2	tablespoons sugar
12	ounces (350 g) rump steak, about $3/4$ inch (2 cm) thick

Sushi Rolls

1	recipe sushi rice (see page 7)
5	nori sheets
2	teaspoons wasabi paste
2	carrots, grated
2	Lebanese cucumbers, seeded and cut into long thin strips
	Storebought or homemade pickled ginger (see page 9), to serve
	Soy sauce, to serve

Serves 4–6 • Preparation 30 minutes + time for the rice + 2–12 hours to marinate • Cooking 10–15 minutes • Difficulty 2

Teriyaki Beef

1. Bring the soy sauce, mirin, and sugar to a boil in a small saucepan over medium heat. Simmer for 2–3 minutes. Remove from heat and let cool.

2. Marinate the steak in the teriyaki sauce in the refrigerator for 2–12 hours. Heat a grill pan and brush with oil. Grill the steak for 3–4 minutes each side. Let cool. Cut into thin strips.

Sushi Rolls

1. Prepare the sushi rice. Lay a nori sheet shiny side down on a bamboo sushi mat. Dip your hands in cold water, and spread with one-fifth of the rice, leaving a $1/2$-inch (1-cm) border on one long side.

2. Spread wasabi lengthwise down the center of the rice. Spread with one-fifth of the beef. Top with the carrot, cucumber, and pickled ginger. Moisten the exposed nori edge with a little water. Using the sushi mat, firmly roll up to enclose the filling. Repeat with the remaining ingredients.

3. Place the rolls seam-side down on a chopping board. Trim the edges with a sharp knife and slice into rounds 1 inch (2.5 cm) thick. Serve with the soy sauce.

RAINBOW sushi rolls

1   recipe California sushi rolls (see page 31)

5   ounces (150 g) sashimi-quality fresh tuna, thinly sliced

2   ounces (60 g) sashimi-quality fresh salmon, thinly sliced

2   ounces (60 g) sashimi-quality fresh white fish fillets, thinly sliced

1   avocado, peeled, pitted, and cut into thin slices

Serves 4–6 • Preparation 30 minutes + time for the rice & sushi rolls
Difficulty 3

1. Prepare the California sushi rolls, but do not slice. First you must wrap the rolls in the slices of fish or avocado.

2. Wrap two of the rolls with the tuna, one with salmon, one with white fish fillets, and with avocado. The rice should be completely covered. Place the rolls seam-side down on a chopping board. Trim the edges with a sharp knife and slice into rounds 1 inch (2.5 cm) thick.

3. Arrange the sushi rolls on individual serving dishes, with a red tuna roll next to a white fish fillet roll, next to a pink salmon roll, next to a green avocado roll, and finishing with another red tuna roll, to obtain a rainbow effect.

AVOCADO sushi rolls

Serves 4–6 • Preparation 30 minutes + time for the rice
Difficulty 2

1	recipe sushi rice (see page 7)	1–2	avocados, peeled, halved, pitted, and sliced into thin strips
5	nori sheets	1/2	cup (120 ml) soy sauce
2 1/2	tablespoons spicy mayonnaise (see page 10)		Wasabi paste, to serve

1. Prepare the sushi rice. Lay a nori sheet shiny side down on a bamboo sushi mat. Dip your hands in cold water, and spread about one-fifth of the rice evenly over the nori sheet, leaving a 1/2-inch (1-cm) border on one long side.

2. Spread with 1/2 tablespoon of spicy mayonnaise. Lay trips of avocado lengthwise down the center of the rice. Lightly moisten the exposed nori edge with a little water. Using the sushi mat, firmly roll up to enclose the filling. Repeat with the remaining ingredients.

3. Place the rolls seam-side down on a chopping board. Trim the edges with a sharp knife and slice into rounds 1 inch (2.5 cm) thick. Serve with the soy sauce and wasabi.

INSIDE-OUT TUNA sushi rolls

Serves 4–6 • Preparation 30 minutes + time for the rice
Difficulty 3

1	recipe sushi rice (see page 7)	2 1/2	tablespoons spicy mayonnaise (see page 10)
5	nori sheets	2 1/2	tablespoons sesame seeds, toasted
4	ounces (125 g) sashimi-quality fresh tuna, cut into long strips	1/3	cup (90 ml) soy sauce, to serve
1	avocado, halved, pitted, and cut into thin strips		Storebought or homemade pickled ginger (see page 9), to serve
1/2	red bell pepper (capsicum) cut into long strips		Wasabi paste, to serve

1. Prepare the sushi rice. Lay a nori sheet shiny side down on a clean work surface. Dip your hands in cold water, and spread one-fifth of the rice evenly over the nori sheet, leaving a 1/2-inch (1-cm) border on one long side. Sprinkle with 1/2 tablespoon of sesame seeds. Turn the nori over and place on a bamboo sushi mat. Spread with 1/2 tablespoon of mayonnaise. Lay strips of tuna, avocado, and bell pepper lengthwise down the center of the nori.

2. Use the sushi mat to firmly roll up and enclose the filling. Repeat with the remaining ingredients. Using a sharp, wet knife, slice the sushi into 1-inch (2.5-cm) thick rounds. Serve with the soy sauce, pickled ginger, and wasabi.

SALMON & AVOCADO sushi rolls

Serves 4–6 • Preparation 30 minutes + time for the rice
Difficulty 2

1	recipe sushi rice (see page 7)	1	small cucumber, peeled and sliced lengthwise into thin strips
5	nori sheets	1/3	cup (90 ml) soy sauce, to serve
4	ounces (125 g) salmon, sliced lengthwise into 1/2-inch (1-cm) strips		Wasabi paste, to serve
1	avocado, halved, pitted, and cut into thin strips		

1. Prepare the sushi rice. Lay a nori sheet shiny side down on a bamboo sushi mat. Dip your hands in cold water, and spread about one-fifth of the rice evenly over the nori sheet, leaving a 1/2-inch (1-cm) border on one long side.

2. Lay strips of salmon, avocado, and cucumber lengthwise down the center of the rice. Lightly moisten the exposed nori edge with a little water. Using the sushi mat, firmly roll up to enclose the filling. Repeat with the remaining ingredients.

3. Place the rolls seam-side down on a chopping board. Trim the edges with a sharp knife and slice into rounds 1 inch (2.5 cm) thick. Serve with the soy sauce and wasabi.

SHRIMP & AVOCADO sushi rolls

Serves 4–6 • Preparation 30 minutes + time for the rice
Difficulty 2

1	recipe sushi rice (see page 7)		and cut in long thin strips
5	sheets nori	16	large cooked shrimp, peeled, deveined, and cut in half lengthwise
1	cucumber, cut in long thin strips		Wasabi paste, to serve
1	avocado, peeled, pitted		

1. Prepare the sushi rice

2. Lay a nori sheet shiny side down on a bamboo sushi mat. Dip your hands in cold water to prevent the rice from sticking, and spread one-fifth of the rice evenly over the nori sheet, leaving a 1/2-inch (1-cm) border on one long side.

3. Lay strips of cucumber, avocado, and shrimp lengthwise down the center of the rice. Lightly moisten the exposed nori edge with a little water. Using the sushi mat, firmly roll up to enclose the filling. Repeat with the remaining ingredients.

4. Place the rolls seam-side down on a chopping board. Trim the edges with a sharp knife and slice into rounds about 1 inch (2.5 cm) thick. Arrange on a platter and serve with the wasabi.

TEX-MEX sushi rolls

1	recipe sushi rice (see page 7)
3	tablespoons very finely chopped fresh parsley
3	tablespoons very finely chopped fresh cilantro (coriander)
2–3	fresh red chilis, seeded and finely chopped
1	cup (120 g) freshly grated Monterey Jack cheese
8–12	large slices, rare cooked roast beef, very thinly sliced
2	cups (500 g) tomato salsa, to serve

Serves 4–6 • Preparation 15 minutes + time for the rice • Difficulty 1

1. Prepare the sushi rice. Mix the parsley, cilantro, chilis, and cheese into the rice.

2. Spread some rice mixture on each slice of roast beef. Roll up sushi-style and slice into 1-inch (2.5-cm) thick rolls.

3. Arrange on a serving platter with the salsa and serve.

TUNA SALAD sushi rolls

1	recipe sushi rice (see page 7)
6	ounces (180 g) canned tuna, drained
1	small red onion, finely chopped
2	tablespoons finely chopped fresh parsley
2-3	tablespoons spicy mayonnaise (see page 10)
1	teaspoon karashi mustard paste
5	nori sheets
	Soy sauce, to serve
	Storebought or homemade pickled ginger (see page 9), to serve

Serves 4-6 • Preparation 30 minutes + time for the rice • Difficulty 2

1. Prepare the sushi rice. Put the tuna in a small bowl and mash with a fork. Add the onion, parsley, mayonnaise, and karashi paste and mix well.

2. Lay a nori sheet shiny side down on a bamboo sushi mat. Dip your hands in cold water to prevent the rice from sticking, and spread one-fifth of the rice evenly over the nori sheet, leaving a $1/2$-inch (1-cm) border on one long side.

3. Spread one-fifth of the tuna salad down the center of the rice. Lightly moisten the exposed nori edge with a little water. Using the sushi mat, firmly roll up to enclose the filling. Repeat with the remaining ingredients.

4. Place the rolls seam-side down on a chopping board. Trim the edges with a sharp knife and slice into rounds about 1 inch (2.5 cm) thick. Serve with the soy sauce and pickled ginger.

You can vary the vegetables in this recipe according to the season and what you have on hand.

ROASTED VEGGIE sushi rolls

1	recipe sushi rice (see page 7)
1	bunch asparagus, with ends chopped off
3	tablespoons extra-virgin olive oil
1	teaspoon salt
4	medium carrots, sliced lengthwise into $1/2$-inch (1-cm) sticks
1	tablespoon maple syrup
1	white onion, thinly sliced
5	nori sheets
	Wasabi paste
	Soy sauce, to serve

Serves 4–6 • Preparation 30 minutes + time for the rice • Cooking 30–40 minutes • Difficulty 2

1. Prepare the sushi rice. Preheat the oven to 400°F (220°C/gas 6).

2. Toss the asparagus with 1 tablespoon of oil and half the salt. Spread out on a baking sheet. Toss the carrots with the maple syrup and 1 tablespoon of oil. Spread out on the baking sheet. Toss the onions with the remaining oil and salt. Spread out on the baking sheet. Roast the vegetables for 30–40 minutes, until they start to brown.

2. Lay a nori sheet shiny side down on a bamboo sushi mat. Dip your hands in cold water to prevent the rice from sticking, and spread one-fifth of the rice evenly over the nori sheet, leaving a $1/2$-inch (1-cm) border on one long side.

4. Spread some wasabi down the center of the rice. Top with one-fifth of the asparagus, carrot, and onion. Moisten the exposed nori edge with a little water. Using the sushi mat, firmly roll up the sushi roll to enclose the filling. Repeat with the remaining ingredients.

5. Place the rolls seam-side down on a chopping board. Trim the edges with a sharp knife and slice into rounds about 1 inch (2.5 cm) thick. Serve with the soy sauce.

JAPANESE OMELET sushi rolls

1/2   recipe sushi rice (see page 7)

Japanese Omelets

2   large eggs
2   teaspoons sugar
1/4   teaspoon salt
3   tablespoons vegetable oil

Sushi Rolls

2   nori sheets
2   teaspoons black sesame seeds
1/3   cup (90 ml) soy sauce, to serve
       Storebought or homemade pickled ginger (see page 9), to serve
       Wasabi paste, to serve

Serves 2–4 • Preparation 20 minutes + time for the rice • Cooking 2–4 minutes • Difficulty 2

1. Prepare the sushi rice.

Japanese Omelets

1. Whisk the eggs, sugar, and salt in a small bowl. Strain through a fine-mesh sieve. Heat 1 1/2 tablespoons of oil in a small omelet pan over high heat. Pour in half the egg mixture, tilting the pan to spread evenly into a thin omelet. Cook until set, 1–2 minutes. Remove from the pan and let cool. Repeat with the remaining egg mixture.

Sushi Rolls

1. Lay a nori sheet shiny side down on a bamboo sushi mat. Lay one of the omelets on top, trimming to fit. Leave a 1/2-inch (1-cm) border on one long side.

2. Dip your hands in cold water, and spread half the rice evenly over the omelet. Sprinkle with half the sesame seeds. Lightly moisten the exposed nori edge with water. Use the sushi mat to firmly roll up and enclose the filling. Repeat with the remaining ingredients.

3. Place the rolls seam-side down on a chopping board. Trim with a sharp knife and slice into rounds 1 inch (2.5 cm) thick. Serve with soy sauce, pickled ginger, and wasabi.

CREAMY CRAB & AVOCADO sushi rolls

1 recipe sushi rice (see page 7)
5 nori sheets
Wasabi paste
8–10 crab sticks (imitation crab), crumbled
2 firm avocados, peeled, pitted and thinly sliced into long strips
5 ounces (150 g) cream cheese, chilled until firm, cut into short batons
2 tablespoons snipped fresh chives
Storebought or homemade pickled ginger (see page 9), to serve

Serves 4–6 • Preparation 30 minutes + time for the rice • Difficulty 2

1. Prepare the sushi rice.

2. Lay a nori sheet shiny side down on a bamboo sushi mat. Dip your hands in cold water to prevent the rice from sticking, and spread one-fifth of the rice evenly over the nori sheet, leaving a $1/2$-inch (1-cm) border on one long side.

3. Spread some wasabi lengthwise down the center of the rice. Lay some pieces of crab stick down the center of the roll. Add strips of avocado and batons of cream cheese. Sprinkle with chives. Lightly moisten the exposed nori edge with a little water. Using the sushi mat, firmly roll up to enclose the filling. Repeat with the remaining ingredients.

4. Place the rolls seam-side down on a chopping board. Trim the edges with a sharp knife and slice into rounds 1 inch (2.5 cm) thick. Serve with the pickled ginger.

Using brown rice to make sushi rolls is a non-traditional but very healthy and delicious alternative to white rice sushi. You will find that the brown rice is less sticky and slightly more tricky to roll but with a little practice it works just as well. Add a nutty flavor to the rice by stirring in 1–2 tablespoons of white sesame seeds along with the vinegar mixture.

TERIYAKI CHICKEN & BROWN RICE sushi rolls

Teriyaki Chicken

4	ounces (120 g) chicken breast fillet, sliced thinly
2	tablespoons teriyaki sauce
1	clove garlic, finely chopped
1	tablespoons peanut oil

Brown Rice Sushi Rolls

1	cup (200 g) brown short-grain rice
2	cups (500 ml) water
2	tablespoons rice vinegar
2	teaspoons sugar
$1/4$	teaspoon salt
3	toasted nori sheets
1	Lebanese cucumber, seeded, cut into matchsticks
$1/2$	cup (25 g) snow pea sprouts, trimmed
$1/3$	cup (90 ml) soy sauce, to serve
	Storebought or homemade pickled ginger (see page 9), to serve

Serves 4 • Preparation 30 minutes + 40 minutes to stand + about 1 hour to cool • Cooking 30 minutes • Difficulty 3

Teriyaki Chicken

1. Combine the chicken, teriyaki sauce and garlic in small bowl. Heat a small frying pan over high heat. Heat the peanut oil. Sauté the chicken until cooked. Let cool.

Sushi Rolls

1. Wash the brown rice under cold running water until the water almost runs clear. Drain for at least 30 minutes.

2. Combine the rice and water in a medium saucepan, cover, and bring to a boil. Reduce the heat and simmer for about 30 minutes, until the water is all absorbed. Remove from the heat. Let stand, covered, for 10 minutes.

3. Combine the rice vinegar, sugar, and salt in a small bowl. Put the rice in a large shallow bowl and gradually stir in the vinegar mixture.

4. Lay a nori sheet shiny side up on a bamboo sushi mat. Dip your hands in cold water to prevent the rice from sticking, and spread one-third of the rice evenly over the nori sheet, leaving a $1/2$-inch (1-cm) border on one long side.

5. Lay a third of the cucumber, sprouts, and chicken in a row down the center of the rice. Lightly moisten the exposed nori edge with a little water. Using the sushi mat, firmly roll up to enclose the filling. Repeat with the remaining ingredients.

6. Place the rolls seam-side down on a chopping board. Trim the edges with a sharp knife and slice into rounds 1 inch (2.5 cm) thick. Serve with the soy sauce and pickled ginger.

INSIDE-OUT SCALLOP & AVOCADO sushi rolls

1 recipe sushi rice (see page 7)

$^1/_2$ tablespoon sesame oil

5 giant scallops, pink corals removed, thinly sliced

Salt and freshly ground black pepper

5 nori sheets

$2^1/_2$ tablespoons spicy mayonnaise (see page 10)

1 avocado, peeled, pitted, and cut into long thin strips

$^1/_3$ cup (90 ml) soy sauce, to serve

Storebought or homemade pickled ginger (see page 9), to serve

Wasabi paste, to serve

Serves 4–6 • Preparation 30 minutes + time for the rice • Cooking 2–3 minutes • Difficulty 2

1. Prepare the sushi rice.

2. Heat the oil in a medium frying pan over medium-high heat until hot. Season the scallop pieces with salt and pepper. Sear in the pan until pale golden brown, 2–3 minutes. Set aside.

3. Lay a nori sheet shiny side down on a clean work surface. Dip your hands in cold water to prevent the rice from sticking, and spread one-fifth of the rice evenly over the nori sheet, leaving a $^1/_2$-inch (1-cm) border on one long side.

4. Quickly turn the nori sheet over and place on a bamboo sushi mat. Spread $^1/_2$ tablespoon of mayonnaise over the nori. Lay pieces of scallop and avocado down the center of the nori sheet. Use the sushi mat to firmly roll up and enclose the filling. Repeat with the remaining ingredients.

5. Place the rolls seam-side down on a chopping board. Trim with a sharp knife and slice into rounds 1 inch (2.5 cm) thick. Serve with soy sauce, pickled ginger, and wasabi.

CALIFORNIA sushi rolls

1 recipe sushi rice (see page 7)
5 nori sheets
2$\frac{1}{2}$ tablespoons mayonnaise
5 ounces (150 g) imitation crab sticks, crumbled
1 avocado, peeled, halved, pitted, and sliced into $\frac{1}{2}$-inch (1-cm) thick, long strips
$\frac{1}{2}$ yellow bell pepper (capsicum) seeded, and sliced lengthwise into $\frac{1}{2}$-inch (1-cm) thick strips
$\frac{1}{3}$ cup (90 ml) soy sauce, to serve
Storebought or homemade pickled ginger (see page 9), to serve
Wasabi paste, to serve

Serves 4–6 • Preparation 30 minutes + time for the rice • Difficulty 2

1. Prepare the sushi rice.

2. Lay a nori sheet shiny side down on a clean work surface. Dip your hands in cold water, and spread one-fifth of the rice evenly over the nori sheet, leaving a $\frac{1}{2}$-inch (1-cm) border on one long side.

3. Quickly turn the nori sheet over and place on a bamboo sushi mat. Spread $\frac{1}{2}$ tablespoon of mayonnaise over the nori. Lay pieces of crab and strips of avocado and bell pepper lengthwise down the center of the nori sheet. Use the sushi mat to firmly roll up and enclose the filling. Repeat with the remaining ingredients.

4. Place the rolls seam-side down on a chopping board. Trim with a sharp knife and slice into rounds 1 inch (2.5 cm) thick. Serve with soy sauce, pickled ginger, and wasabi.

For this recipe you will need 12 bamboo skewers, broken in half, to skewer the shrimp so that they don't curl up during frying. If they curl, you won't be able to insert them in the sushi rolls.

TEMPURA SHRIMP sushi rolls

$^1/_2$ recipe sushi rice (see page 7)

Tempura Shrimp

1   large egg, separated

1   tablespoon freshly squeezed lemon juice

$^2/_3$ cup (150 ml) iced water

$^1/_3$ cup (50 g) all-purpose (plain) flour

24   large uncooked shrimp (prawns)

2   cups (500 ml) peanut oil, for frying

Sushi Rolls

2   nori sheets

1-2   teaspoons wasabi paste

$^1/_2$ cup (25 g) mizuna or baby spinach leaves

$^1/_3$ cup (90 ml) soy sauce, to serve

Storebought or homemade pickled ginger (see page 9), to serve

Wasabi paste, to serve

Serves 4 • Preparation 30 minutes + time for the rice • Cooking 10 minutes • Difficulty 3

1. Prepare the sushi rice.

Tempura Shrimp

1. Beat the egg yolk, lemon juice, water, and flour in a small bowl until just smooth. Beat the egg white in a separate bowl until stiff. Fold it into the egg yolk batter.

2. Skewer each shrimp lengthwise down the center on half a bamboo skewer to keep it straight during cooking.

3. Heat the peanut oil in a large wok until it reaches 375°F (190°F) on a frying thermometer. If you do not have a frying thermometer, drop a small piece of bread into the hot oil. If it immediately bubbles to the surface and turns golden, the oil is ready.

4. Dip the shrimp into the batter, then let drain of the excess. Fry in small batches until golden brown, 2–3 minutes. Drain on paper towels.

Sushi Rolls

1. Cut the nori sheets in half crosswise and then cut into $1^1/_4$-inch (3-cm) strips. Spread 1 tablespoon of rice over each piece of nori, top with a tempura shrimp, a little wasabi, and 2–3 leaves of mizuna or baby spinach. Roll up carefully to secure the filling. Lightly moisten the ends of the nori with water to make them stick together. Repeat until all the ingredients are used.

2. Arrange on a serving platter and serve with soy sauce, pickled ginger, and wasabi.

PICKLED DAIKON thin sushi rolls

1   recipe sushi rice (see page 7)
8   (7-inch/18-cm) long thin strips
     pickled daikon
4   nori sheets
     Wasabi paste
4   teaspoons toasted white
     sesame seeds
     Soy sauce, to serve

Serves 4–6 • Preparation 30 minutes + time for the rice • Difficulty 2

1. Prepare the sushi rice. Sprinkle the strips of daikon lightly with salt. Set aside for 15 minutes. Rinse the daikon in cold water and dry with paper towels.

2. Lightly toast the nori sheets over a very low gas flame or electric hotplate. Cut each nori sheet in half lengthwise.

3. Lay a nori sheet shiny side down on a bamboo sushi mat. Dip your hands in cold water to prevent the rice from sticking, and spread one-eighth of the rice evenly over the nori sheet, leaving a $1/2$-inch (1-cm) border on one long side.

4. Spread some wasabi lengthwise down the center of the rice. Cover evenly with the daikon. Sprinkle with sesame seeds. Lightly moisten the exposed nori edge with a little water. Using the sushi mat, firmly roll up and enclose the filling. Repeat with the remaining ingredients.

5. Place the rolls seam-side down on a chopping board. Trim the edges with a sharp knife and slice into rounds 1 inch (2.5 cm) thick. Serve with the soy sauce.

CUCUMBER thin sushi rolls

1 recipe sushi rice (see page 7)
4 nori sheets
1–2 tablespoons finely grated
wasabi horseradish
1 cucumber, with peel, cut into
quarters lengthwise
Soy sauce, to serve

Serves 4–6 • Preparation 30 minutes + time for the rice • Difficulty 2

1. Prepare the sushi rice. Lightly toast the nori sheets over a very low gas flame or electric hotplate. Cut each nori sheet in half lengthwise.

2. Lay a nori sheet shiny side down on a bamboo sushi mat. Dip your hands in cold water to prevent the rice from sticking, and spread one-eighth of the rice evenly over the nori sheet, leaving a $1/2$-inch (1-cm) border on one long side.

3. Spread some wasabi horseradish lengthwise down the center of the rice. Cover with the cucumber quarters. Lightly moisten the exposed nori edge with a little water. Using the sushi mat, firmly roll up the sushi roll to enclose the filling. Repeat with the remaining ingredients.

4. Place the rolls seam-side down on a chopping board. Trim the edges with a sharp knife and slice into rounds 1 inch (2.5 cm) thick. Serve with the soy sauce.

In this recipe, the natural rounds of the squids' bodies are used to form the sushi rolls. These pretty rolls are perfect for special occasions.

STUFFED SQUID sushi rolls

2	medium squid, cleaned
3	tablespoons saké
3	tablespoons Japanese rice wine vinegar
2	tablespoons sugar
1	tablespoon mirin
2	tablespoons soy sauce
2	ounces (60 g) ground (minced) chicken breast
1	tablespoon peeled and finely chopped fresh ginger
1/2	recipe sushi rice (see page 7)
	Storebought or homemade pickled ginger (see page 9), to serve

Serves 4 • Preparation 45 minutes + time for the rice • Cooking 5–10 minutes • Difficulty 3

1. Peel the skin off the squid by holding the two flaps and peeling down the body. Put the squid bodies in a saucepan with 1 tablespoon each of saké and rice vinegar. Cover with boiling water. Simmer for 1–2 minutes. Do not overcook, as the squid will become rubbery. Drain, then drizzle with the remaining rice vinegar. Chop the flaps and tentacles.

2. Combine the remaining 2 tablespoons of saké, the sugar, mirin, and soy sauce in a saucepan over medium heat and bring to a boil. Add the chicken, the chopped squid, and the ginger. Stir with a fork until the meat turns white. Using a slotted spoon, transfer the cooked meat to another bowl, leaving the juice in the saucepan. Boil the juice over high heat until thickened, 1–2 minutes. Stir the meat back in to absorb the juice, then remove from the heat.

3. Prepare the sushi rice. Stir the warm rice mixture into the meat. Stuff each squid with the rice mixture. Cut into six slices. Arrange on plates and serve with pickled ginger.

If you liked this recipe, you will love these as well.

RAINBOW sushi rolls

CREAMY CRAB & AVOCADO sushi rolls

TEMPURA SHRIMP sushi rolls

CRABMEAT thin sushi rolls

1   recipe sushi rice (see page 7)
5   ounces (150 g) crab meat
4   nori sheets
3–4   tablespoons spicy mayonnaise
       (see page 10)
       Soy sauce, to serve

Serves 4–6 • Preparation 30 minutes + time for the rice • Difficulty 2

1. Prepare the sushi rice. Lightly toast the nori sheet over a very low gas flame or electric hotplate. Cut each nori sheet in half lengthwise.

2. Lay a nori sheet shiny side down on a bamboo sushi mat. Dip your hands in cold water to prevent the rice from sticking, and spread one-eighth of the rice evenly over the nori sheet, leaving a $1/2$-inch (1-cm) border on one long side.

3. Spread some spicy mayonnaise lengthwise down the center of the rice. Spread the mayonnaise evenly with the crab meat. Lightly moisten the exposed nori edge with a little water. Using the sushi mat, firmly roll up and enclose the filling. Repeat with the remaining ingredients.

4. Place the rolls seam-side down on a chopping board. Trim the edges with a sharp knife and slice into rounds 1 inch (2.5 cm) thick. Serve with the soy sauce.

SALMON thin sushi rolls

1 recipe sushi rice (see page 7)
5 ounces (150 g) sashimi-quality skinless salmon fillet, cut into long thin strips
4 nori sheets
    Wasabi paste
    Soy sauce, to serve

Serves 4–6 • Preparation 30 minutes + time for the rice • Difficulty 2

1. Prepare the sushi rice. Lightly toast the nori sheets over a very low gas flame or electric hotplate. Cut each nori sheet in half lengthwise.

2. Lay a nori sheet shiny side down on a bamboo sushi mat. Dip your hands in cold water to prevent the rice from sticking, and spread one-eighth of the rice evenly over the nori sheet, leaving a $1/2$-inch (1-cm) border on one long side.

3. Spread some wasabi lengthwise down the center of the rice. Spread the wasabi evenly with the salmon. Lightly moisten the exposed nori edge with a little water. Using the sushi mat, firmly roll up and enclose the filling. Repeat with the remaining ingredients.

4. Place the rolls seam-side down on a chopping board. Trim the edges with a sharp knife and slice into rounds 1 inch (2.5 cm) thick. Serve with the soy sauce.

Quinoa is a grain-like food, originally from the Andes region of South America, which is prized for its nutritional qualities.

QUINOA sushi rolls

2	cups (400 g) quinoa
5 1/2	cups (1.37 liters) water
1/3	cup (90 ml) + 2 tablespoons rice vinegar
2	tablespoons sugar
2	teaspoons salt
1/3	cup (90 ml) soy sauce
1	sweet potato, peeled and cut into x 2 1/2 x 1/4-inch (60 x 5-mm) batons
5	ounces (150 g) green beans, trimmed
1	tablespoon butter
1	tablespoon sesame oil
1	white onion, finely chopped
5	ounces (150 g) cream cheese, chilled until firm, cut into 2 x 1/4-inch (50 x 5-mm) batons
1/2	cup (120 ml) spicy mayonnaise (see page 10)
6	nori sheets
2	tablespoons chopped fresh cilantro (coriander)

Serves 4–6 • Preparation 30 minutes + about 1 hour to cool • Cooking 35 minutes • Difficulty 2

1. Put the quinoa in a pot with 4 cups (1 liter) of water. Bring to a boil, cover, and simmer until tender, 15–20 minutes.

2. Stir 2 tablespoons of rice vinegar, the sugar and salt in a small bowl until the sugar and salt have dissolved. Drain the quinoa, then stir in the vinegar mixture, tossing to mix. Set aside to cool.

3. Bring the remaining 1 1/2 cups (375 ml) of water, soy sauce, and remaining 1/3 cup (90 ml) of rice vinegar to a boil. Add the sweet potatoes and green beans and cook until tender, 8–10 minutes. Drain well.

4. Heat the butter and oil in a small frying pan over medium heat. Add the onion and sauté until pale gold. Set aside.

5. Lay a sheet of nori shiny side down on a clean work surface. Dip your hands in cold water to prevent the quinoa from sticking, and spread a quarter of the quinoa mixture evenly over the nori sheet, leaving a 1/2-inch (1-cm) border on one long side.

6. Spread 1 tablespoon of spicy mayonnaise and some caramelized onion lengthwise down the center of the quinoa. Lay the batons of sweet potato and cream cheese, and the green beans over the top.Use the sushi mat to firmly roll up and enclose the filling. Repeat with the remaining ingredients.

7. Place the rolls seam-side down on a chopping board. Trim the edges with a sharp knife and slice into rounds 1 inch (2.5 cm) thick. Garnish with the cilantro and serve.

INSIDE-OUT VEGETARIAN sushi rolls

1   recipe sushi rice (see page 7)

5   nori sheets

$^1/_3$ cup (90 ml) spicy mayonnaise (see page 10)

1   small cucumber, with peel, trimmed and cut into long thin strips

2   avocados, peeled, pitted, and cut into thin strips

1   (12-ounce/350-g) jar red bell peppers (capsicums), cut in thin strips

Serves 4–6 • Preparation 30 minutes + time for the rice • Difficulty 3

1. Prepare the sushi rice.

2. Lay a sheet of nori shiny side down on a clean work surface. Dip your hands in cold water to prevent the rice from sticking, and spread one-fifth of the rice evenly over the nori sheet, leaving a $^1/_2$-inch (1-cm) border on one long side.

3. Quickly turn the nori sheet over and place on a bamboo sushi mat. Spread some mayonnaise on the nori. Lay strips of cucumber, avocado, and bell pepper lengthwise down the center. Use the sushi mat to firmly roll up and enclose the filling. Repeat with the remaining ingredients.

4. Place the rolls seam-side down on a chopping board. Trim the edges with a sharp knife and slice into rounds 1 inch (2.5 cm) thick. Arrange on a platter and serve.

INSIDE-OUT CARROT & AVOCADO sushi rolls

1   recipe sushi rice (see page 7)
5   nori sheets
2½ tablespoons black sesame seeds, toasted
    Wasabi paste
1   small cucumber, with peel, trimmed and cut into long thin strips
2   avocados, peeled, pitted, and cut into thin strips
2   carrots, cut into long thin strips
    Storebought or homemade pickled ginger (see page 9), to serve

Serves 4–6 • Preparation 30 minutes + time for the rice • Difficulty 3

1. Prepare the sushi rice.

2. Lay a sheet of nori shiny side down on a clean work surface. Dip your hands in cold water to prevent the rice from sticking, and spread one-fifth of the rice evenly over the nori sheet, leaving a ½-inch (1-cm) border on one long side. Sprinkle with ½ tablespoon of the sesame seeds.

3. Quickly turn the nori sheet over and place on a bamboo sushi mat. Dab some wasabi on the nori. Lay strips of cucumber, avocado, and carrots lengthwise down the center of the nori sheet. Use the sushi mat to firmly roll up and enclose the filling. Repeat with the remaining ingredients.

4. Place the rolls seam-side down on a chopping board. Trim the edges with a sharp knife and slice into rounds 1 inch (2.5 cm) thick. Arrange on a platter and serve with the pickled ginger.

44

MANGO & COCONUT sushi rolls

2   cups (400 g) Japanese sushi rice (short-grain sticky rice)

1/3   cup (90 ml) coconut milk

2   teaspoons sugar

1   teaspoon freshly squeezed lime juice

      Pinch of salt

2   mangoes, peeled, pitted, and cut into long strips

1   cucumber, with peel, cut in long strips

4   nori sheets

Serves 4–6 • Preparation 30 minutes + 1 hour to cool • Cooking 15 minutes • Difficulty 2

1. Steam the rice until just tender over lightly salted water. Place the hot rice in a large bowl.

2. Combine the coconut milk, sugar, lime juice, and salt in a bowl and stir until the sugar has dissolved.

3. Drizzle the coconut milk mixture evenly over the rice and mix until well combined. Let cool to room temperature.

4. Lay a sheet of nori shiny side down on a clean work surface. Dip your hands in cold water to prevent the rice from sticking, and spread a quarter of the rice evenly over the nori sheet, leaving a 1/2-inch (1-cm) border on one long side. Place strips of mango and cucumber down the center of the rice. Use the sushi mat to firmly roll up and enclose the filling. Repeat with the remaining ingredients.

5. Place the rolls seam-side down on a chopping board. Trim the ends with a sharp knife and slice into rounds 1 inch (2.5 cm) thick. Arrange on a platter and serve.

If you liked this recipe, you will love these as well.

SALMON SUSHI ROLLS
with passionfruit sauce

TEX-MEX sushi rolls

QUINOA sushi rolls

pressed & rolled sushi

VEGETARIAN sushi cones

½ recipe sushi rice (see page 7)

5 nori sheets, cut in half

Chili sauce, storebought or homemade (see page 10)

5 ounces (150 g) cream cheese, chilled until firm, cut into short batons

1 cucumber, with peel, seeds removed, cut into long thin strips

2 carrots, cut into long thin strips

1 red bell pepper (capsicum), cut into long thin strips

2 tablespoons white sesame seeds

Soy sauce, to serve

Wasabi paste, to serve

Storebought or homemade pickled ginger (see page 9), to serve

Serves 4–6 • Preparation 20 minutes + time for the rice • Difficulty 1

1. Prepare the sushi rice.

2. Place a nori sheet shiny side down in one hand. Spread 3–4 tablespoons of sushi rice in a thin layer over one half of the nori sheet. Dab with some chili sauce. Top with a few batons of cream cheese. Cover with strips of cucumber, carrot, and bell pepper, placing them diagonally across the rice. Sprinkle with some sesame seeds.

3. Roll the nori around the filling to create a cone by folding the bottom left-hand corner of the nori sheet toward the top right-hand corner and rolling. Lightly moisten the corner of the nori sheet and press down to seal.

4. Repeat with the remaining ingredients to make ten cones. Serve with the soy sauce, wasabi, and pickled ginger.

If you liked this recipe, you will love these as well.

78

SMOKED SALMON & VEGGIE sushi cones

80

BROWN RICE & SHRIMP sushi cones

81

TUNA & VEGGIE sushi cones

You will need a rectangular *oshibako*, or wooden sushi mold, for this recipe. It should measure about 7 x 5 x 2 inches (18 x 13 x 5 cm). Soak the wooden mold in cold water for about 30 minutes before you start.

CLASSIC MACKEREL pressed sushi

1½   pounds (750 g) mackerel fillets, with skin
1   cup (200 g) coarse sea salt
1   recipe sushi rice (see page 7)
1   cup (250 ml) Japanese rice wine vinegar
¼   cup (60 ml) water
1   tablespoon sugar
1   tablespoon mirin
Wasabi paste

Serves 4–6 • Preparation 45 minutes + time for the rice + 4–5 hours to drain & marinate • Difficulty 2

1. Lay the mackerel fillets in a large shallow bowl and sprinkle with the salt. Carefully rub the fillets with the salt. Transfer to a colander and let drain for 3–4 hours. Rinse carefully to remove excess salt and dry with a clean kitchen towel.

2. Prepare the sushi rice. Soak the sushi mold in cold water for 30 minutes.

3. Mix the rice vinegar, water, sugar, and mirin in a large plastic bowl, stirring until the sugar is dissolved. Add the mackerel and let marinate for 1 hour. The flesh will turn very white. Remove the fillets from the marinade and carefully remove the thin outer skin from the fish. Leave the iridescent underskin on the fish.

4. Transfer the fillets to a chopping board. Run your fingertips light over the fish, feeling for bones. Use tweezers to remove any bones. Trim the edges to even.

5. Place half the mackerel fillets skin-side down in the sushi mold. Fill in any gaps with pieces of mackerel offcuts. Dot with some wasabi here and there. Top with half of the sushi rice. Press the sushi mold lid to compress the sushi.

6. Invert to remove the sushi. Cut into four even pieces crosswise and in half lengthwise to yield eight pieces. Repeat with the remaining ingredients to yield sixteen sushi rectangles. Keep the sushi in the refrigerator until ready to serve.

SMOKED CHICKEN & GREEN APPLE
pressed sushi

1   recipe sushi rice (see page 7)

6   ounces (180 g) thinly sliced
    smoked chicken

    Sweet chili sauce, storebought
    or homemade (see page 10)

1   large, organic Granny Smith
    apple, with peel, cored, and
    sliced paper thin

    Seaweed salad, to serve

Serves 4–6 • Preparation 20 minutes + time for the rice • Difficulty 1

1. Prepare the sushi rice. Soak a sushi mold in cold water for 30 minutes.

2. Line the sushi mold with half the smoked chicken. Cover with a quarter of the rice in an even layer. Dab with chili sauce here and there. Top with a layer of half of the apple slices. Cover with a quarter of the rice. Press the sushi mold lid to compress and mold the sushi.

3. Invert to remove the sushi. Cut into four even pieces crosswise, then in half lengthwise to yield eight pieces. Repeat with the remaining ingredients to yield sixteen sushi rectangles. Keep the sushi in the refrigerator until ready to serve. Serve with extra chili sauce and seaweed salad.

YELLOWFIN & FLYING FISH ROE
pressed sushi

1 recipe sushi rice (see page 7)
10 ounces (300 g) sashimi-quality yellowtail, thinly sliced against the grain
5 teaspoons flying fish roe
  Wasabi paste

Serves 4–6 • Preparation 20 minutes + time for the rice • Difficulty 1

1. Prepare the sushi rice. Soak a sushi mold in cold water for 30 minutes.

2. Arrange a layer of yellowtail in the sushi mold. Spread evenly with half the fish roe and dab with wasabi here and there. Top with half of the sushi rice. Press the sushi mold lid to compress and mold the sushi.

3. Invert to remove the sushi. Cut into four even pieces crosswise, then in half lengthwise to yield eight pieces. Repeat with the remaining ingredients to yield sixteen sushi rectangles. Keep the sushi in the refrigerator until ready to serve.

HAM & AVOCADO pressed sushi

Serves 4-6 • Preparation 20 minutes + time for the rice
Difficulty 1

1	recipe sushi rice (see page 7)		pitted, and very thinly sliced
5	ounces (150 g) thinly sliced prosciutto crudo		Wasabi paste
2	small, firm-ripe avocados, peeled,		Brine-cured capers, drained, to decorate

1. Prepare the sushi rice. Soak a sushi mold in cold water for 30 minutes.

2. Line the sushi mold with half the prosciutto. Cover with a layer of half the avocado slices. Dab with wasabi here and there. Top with half of the sushi rice. Press the sushi mold lid to compress and mold the sushi.

3. Invert to remove the sushi. Cut into four even pieces crosswise, then in half lengthwise to yield eight pieces. Repeat with the remaining ingredients to yield sixteen sushi rectangles.

4. Decorate each piece with one or two capers. Keep the sushi in the refrigerator until ready to serve.

SHRIMP nigiri

Serves 4-6 • Preparation 20 minutes + time for the rice
Cooking 2-3 minutes • Difficulty 2

1	recipe sushi rice (see page 7)	1	tablespoon wasabi paste + extra if liked
24	medium-large shrimp (prawns)	1/3	cup (90 ml) soy sauce to serve

1. Prepare the sushi rice.

2. Remove the heads from the shrimp and devein. Beginning at the tail end, push a long skewer through each one between the flesh and the shell, to prevent it from curling.

3. Fill a large frying pan with water and bring to a boil. Cook the shrimp in the pan until they change color, 2-3 minutes. Remove and plunge into a bowl of cold water to stop the cooking process. Drain on paper towels. Set aside for 5 minutes to cool.

4. Carefully remove the skewers from the shrimp. Peel, leaving the tails intact. Butterfly the shrimp, cutting from underneath.

5. Divide the rice into 24 even-size balls. Shape the balls, using wet hands, to prevent the rice from sticking, into brick shaped logs. Smear the tops with a little wasabi and lay a shrimp on top. Serve with soy sauce and extra wasabi.

SALMON & CRAB pressed sushi

Serves 4-6 • Preparation 20 minutes + time for the rice
Difficulty 1

1	recipe sushi rice (see page 7)	5	ounces (150 g) canned crab
10	ounces (300 g) sashimi-quality salmon, thinly sliced against the grain		Wasabi paste
		5	teaspoons mayonnaise

1. Prepare the sushi rice. Soak a sushi mold in cold water for 30 minutes.

2. Arrange a layer of salmon in the sushi mold. Spread evenly with a layer of half the crab. Dab with wasabi and spread with half the mayonnaise. Top with half of the sushi rice. Press the sushi mold lid to compress and mold the sushi.

3. Invert to remove the sushi. Cut into four even pieces crosswise, then in half lengthwise to yield eight pieces. Repeat with the remaining ingredients to yield sixteen sushi rectangles. Keep the sushi in the refrigerator until ready to serve.

CRAB & AVOCADO pressed sushi

Serves 4-6 • Preparation 20 minutes + time for the rice
Difficulty 1

1	recipe sushi rice (see page 7)		peeled, pitted and thinly sliced
8	ounces (250 g) imitation crab meat sticks or rolls, shredded		Wasabi paste
			Lime slices, to garnish
2	firm-ripe avocados,		Soy sauce, to serve

1. Prepare the sushi rice. Soak s sushi mold in cold water for 30 minutes.

2. Line the sushi mold with a layer of imitation crab. Cover with a layer of avocado. Dab with wasabi here and there. Cover with a layer of half the rice. Press the sushi mold lid to compress and mold the sushi.

3. Invert to remove the sushi. Cut into four even pieces crosswise, then in half lengthwise to yield eight pieces. Repeat with the remaining ingredients to yield sixteen sushi rectangles.

4. Keep the sushi in the refrigerator until ready to serve. Garnish with the lime and serve with the soy sauce for dipping.

SHRIMP & NORI pressed sushi

1	recipe sushi rice (see page 7)
24	medium-large shrimp (prawns)
	Wasabi paste
2	nori sheets
	Soy sauce, to serve

Serves 4–6 • Preparation 20 minutes + time for the rice • Difficulty 2

1. Prepare the sushi rice. Soak a sushi mold in cold water for 30 minutes.

2. Remove the heads, shells, and tails from the shrimp. Turn upside down and cut lengthwise down the bellies. Remove the dark vein and open the shrimp out flat.

3. Arrange a first layer of opened-out shrimp in the sushi mold, with the rounded orange side facing downward. Dab with wasabi here and there. Top with a quarter of the sushi rice. Cut one nori sheet to fit the mold and place in the mold. Cover with another quarter of the rice. Press the sushi mold lid to compress and mold the sushi.

4. Invert to remove and cut into four even pieces crosswise, then in half lengthwise to yield eight pieces. Repeat with the remaining ingredients to yield sixteen sushi rectangles. Serve with soy sauce for dipping.

SMOKED SALMON sushi squares

1   nori sheet
¹/₂   recipe sushi rice (see page 7)
1   teaspoon wasabi paste
2   tablespoons spicy mayonnaise
      (see page 10)
8   large slices smoked salmon
¹/₄   cup (60 ml) water
1   tablespoon rice vinegar
      Pickled cucumber garnish
      (see page 10)

Serves 4 • Preparation 20 minutes + time for the rice + 1 hour to chill
Difficulty 2

1. Prepare the sushi rice. Line an 8-inch (20-cm) square cake pan with plastic wrap (cling film) leaving plenty of overhang on two sides. Line the base with a sheet of nori.

2. Press the cooled sushi rice into the prepared cake pan and using a second piece of plastic wrap and your hands, smooth the rice out until it is completely flat.

3. Spread with the wasabi and mayonnaise. Lay the smoked salmon on top, trimming to fit. Refrigerate for 1 hour.

4. Combine the water and rice vinegar in a small bowl. Remove the chilled rice from the pan using the overhanging plastic wrap. Dip the tip of a knife into the water mixture and cut the slab of sushi into 2-inch (5-cm) squares. Top each square of sushi with some pickled cucumber and serve.

These "moneybags" look very pretty and will add to any sushi platter.

SUSHI OMELET money bags

1/2	recipe sushi rice (see page 7)
5	dried shiitake mushrooms
1	tablespoon mirin
1 1/2	tablespoons cornstarch (cornflour)
1/4	cup (60 ml) water
4	large eggs + 4 large egg yolks
1	teaspoon salt
4	tablespoons (60 ml) vegetable oil
3	tablespoons black sesame seeds
8–10	chives, to tie the moneybags

Serves 4 • Preparation 20 minutes + time for the rice + 4 hours to soak
Cooking 25–30 minutes • Difficulty 3

1. Prepare the sushi rice.

2. Soak the mushrooms in 1 cup (250 ml) of warm water for 4 hours. Place in a small saucepan with the reserved soaking water over medium heat and bring to a boil. Stir in the mirin. Remove from the heat and let cool in the liquid. Slice thinly.

3. Put the cornstarch in a small bowl and stir in the water. Add the eggs, egg yolks, and salt and stir well. Heat 1 tablespoon of oil in a 7-inch (18-cm) frying pan. Add enough of the mixture to coat the bottom of the pan and cook over medium heat until just set. Turn the omelet and cook the other side. Place on a plate. Cook the rest of the egg batter in the same way. You will get eight to ten thin omelets.

4. Toast the sesame seeds over medium in a small frying pan, 2–3 minutes. Stir the sesame seeds and mushrooms into the rice.

5. Take large handfuls of the rice mixture and squeeze into balls. Place in the center of an omelet and carefully draw the edges of the omelet up around the ball of rice, bringing them together at the top in the shape of an old-fashioned moneybag. Tie with a chive and carefully place on a serving platter. Repeat with the remaining ingredients.

VALENTINE'S DAY pressed sushi

1	recipe sushi rice (see page 7)
4	ounces (120 g) sashimi-grade bluefin tuna, thinly sliced
	Wasabi paste
12	perilla leaves + extra, to garnish

Serves 4–6 • Preparation 15 minutes + time for the rice + 30 minutes to rest • Difficulty 1

1. Prepare the sushi rice.

2. Line a heart-shaped cake pan with plastic wrap (cling film). Cover with a layer of tuna, followed by a layer of perilla leaves. Dab with wasabi and cover with enough rice to fill the pan. Press it down gently but firmly with your fingertips. Fold the plastic wrap over the top and cover with a heavy weight. Let rest for 30 minutes.

3. Carefully turn the sushi-heart out of the pan. Remove the plastic wrap and bring to the table. Garnish the dish with extra perilla leaves. Cut into twelve small squares to serve.

SMOKED SALMON onigiri

1   recipe sushi rice (see page 7)
3   ounces (90 g) smoked salmon
    slices, finely chopped
1   teaspoon wasabi paste
1   nori sheet, cut into
    1 x 3-inch (2.5 x 8-cm) strips
¼   cup (60 ml) soy sauce,
    for dipping

Serves 4–6 • Preparation 20 minutes + time for the rice • Difficulty 1

1. Prepare the sushi rice.

2. Mix the salmon and wasabi in a small bowl and set aside. Dip your hands in cold water to prevent the rice from sticking, and shape the rice into balls the size of golf balls. Make a hollow in the center and fill with 1 teaspoon of the salmon mixture. Form another ball the same size and place on top, then mold them together. Flatten the balls and shape them into a triangle, about 1 inch (2.5 cm) thick and 3 inches (8 cm) high.

3. Wrap strips of nori under the bases of the rice triangles, smoothing them evenly up the sides. Serve with soy sauce for dipping.

SMOKED SALMON pressed sushi

1   recipe sushi rice (see page 7)
1   unwaxed lime, sliced paper thin, halved
8   ounces (250 g) smoked salmon
    Wasabi paste
    Storebought or homemade pickled ginger (see page 9), to serve

Serves 4–6 • Preparation 20 minutes + time for the rice • Difficulty 2

1. Prepare the sushi rice.

2. Partially line the sushi mold with half slices of lime. Cover with a layer of half the smoked salmon. Dab with wasabi here and there. Top with half of the sushi rice. Press the sushi mold lid to compress and mold the sushi.

3. Invert to remove and cut into four even pieces crosswise, then in half lengthwise to yield eight pieces. Repeat with the remaining ingredients to yield sixteen sushi rectangles. Keep the sushi in the refrigerator until ready to serve. Serve with the pickled ginger.

SMOKED SALMON & MANGO *nigiri*

1   recipe sushi rice (see page 7)

1   mango, peeled, pitted, and cut into 32 small cubes

8   ounces (250 g) smoked salmon slices

     Wasabi paste

     Storebought or homemade pickled ginger (see page 9), to serve

     Citrus dipping sauce (see page 10), to serve

Serves 4–6 • Preparation 15 minutes + time for the rice • Difficulty 1

1. Prepare the sushi rice.

2. Dip your hands in cold water to prevent the rice from sticking, and place 2 tablespoons of the cooled sushi rice in the palm of one hand. Squeeze it a little then make a hole with your thumb and put a piece of mango inside. Squeeze the rice around the mango and shape into an oblong.

3. Slice the salmon into pieces just large enough to drape over the oblongs.

4. Put a tiny ball of wasabi on top of each rice oblong and drape a piece of smoked salmon over each one.

5. Serve with the pickled ginger and citrus dipping sauce.

Nigiri, or "hand-formed" sushi is made by pressing sushi rice into an oblong ball, dabbing the top with a little wasabi, and draping a topping such as salmon or omelet over each oblong. Sometimes the topping is strapped to the rice using a strip of nori.

JAPANESE OMELET nigiri

$1/2$	recipe sushi rice (see page 7)
4	large eggs
2	tablespoons sugar
1	teaspoon soy sauce
1	tablespoon butter
	Wasabi paste
2	sheets nori

Serves 4 • Preparation 30 minutes + time for the rice • Cooking 5 minutes • Difficulty 2

1. Prepare the sushi rice.

2. Crack the eggs into a bowl and whisk until smooth. Add the sugar and soy sauce, stirring until well mixed.

3. Heat a large frying pan over medium heat. Add the butter and tilt the pan so that it spreads evenly over the bottom. Pour the egg mixture into the pan.

4. When the egg looks opaque and you can get a spatula under it without tearing the omelet, flip it and cook the other side.

5. When cooked through and pale golden brown on the bottom, remove the omelet from the pan. Slice into $1^{1}/_{2}$ x $2^{1}/_{2}$-inch (4 x 6-cm) strips.

6. Dip your hands in cold water to prevent the rice from sticking, and place 2 tablespoons of the cooled sushi rice in the palm of one hand. Dab a tiny ball of wasabi on top of each rice oblong and place a piece of omelet on top.

7. Cut the nori sheets into $1/4$-inch (5-mm) wide strips. Wrap a strip of nori around each piece of nigiri, cutting to fit and sticking the ends together underneath with cold water.

NIGIRI platter

1   recipe sushi rice (see page 7)
     Wasabi paste
5   ounces (150 g) sashimi-grade
     albacore tuna
5   ounces (150 g) sashimi-grade
     sea bream
5   ounces (150 g) sashimi-grade
     red snapper
5   ounces (150 g) sashimi-grade
     salmon
     Storebought or homemade
     pickled ginger (see page 9),
     to serve

Serves 4–6 • Preparation 30 minutes + time for the rice • Difficulty 1

1. Prepare the sushi rice.

2. Lay all the fish on a chopping board and check for bones
    with your fingertips. Remove any bones with tweezers.
    Thinly slice the fish into pieces measuring about 1 x 2 inches
    (2.5 x 5 cm).

3. Dip your hands in cold water to prevent the rice from
    sticking, and place 2 tablespoons of the cooled sushi rice in
    the palm of one hand. Dab the top of the rice oblong with
    wasabi and fit a piece of fish over the top. Squeeze gently
    to keep in place and mold the fish over the rice. Place on a
    large platter. Repeat with all the rice and fish.

4. Serve with pickled ginger and one of our sushi sauces
    (see page 10).

GRILLED BELL PEPPER *nigiri*

½   recipe sushi rice (see page 7)

1   small red bell pepper (capsicum), seeded and cut into 4–6 strips

1   small yellow bell pepper (capsicum), seeded and cut into 4–6 strips

     Wasabi paste

2   nori sheets

     Seaweed salad, to serve

Serves 4–6 • Preparation 30 minutes + time for the rice • Cooking 10–15 minutes • Difficulty 1

1. Prepare the sushi rice.

2. To prepare the bell peppers, preheat a grill pan or overhead broiler (grill) in the oven. Grill the bell peppers until the skins are blackened and charred. Place in a plastic food bag and let sweat for 10 minutes. Remove from the bag and peel off all the chared skin. Slice the bell peppers into $1\frac{1}{2}$ x $2\frac{1}{2}$-inch (4 x 6-cm) strips.

3. Dip your hands in cold water to prevent the rice from sticking, and place of the cooled sushi rice in the palm of one hand. Dab the top of the rice oblong with wasabi and fit a piece of bell pepper over the top. Repeat with all the rice and bell peppers.

4. Cut the nori sheets into $\frac{1}{2}$-inch (1-cm) wide strips. Wrap a strip of nori around each piece of nigiri, cutting to fit, sticking the ends together underneath with cold water. Serve with the seaweed salad.

Battleship sushi, known in Japan as *gunkanmaki*, is a special type of nigiri (hand-formed sushi). You can fill the warships with many different fillings, including fish roe, cooked quail eggs, corn, oysters, and chopped smoked salmon, to mention a few.

BATTLESHIP SUSHI with teriyaki chicken

1	recipe sushi rice (see page 7)
5	nori sheets
$\frac{1}{4}$	cup (60 ml) dark soy sauce
$\frac{1}{4}$	cup (60 ml) saké
2	teaspoons sugar
14	ounces (400 g) boneless, skinless chicken breast, sliced into thin strips
	Storebought or homemade sweet chili sauce (see page 10), to garnish
	Snipped fresh chives
	Storebought or homemade spicy mayonnaise (see page 10), to garnish
	Capers, to garnish

Serves 4–6 • Preparation 30 minutes + time for the rice + 30 minutes to marinate • Cooking 10 minutes • Difficulty 2

1. Prepare the sushi rice. Cut each nori sheet into six equal strips.

2. Combine the soy sauce, saké, and sugar in a small bowl and mix well. Place the chicken in a large bowl and pour the soy sauce mixture over the top. Mix gently to coat all over and set aside to marinate for 30 minutes.

3. Preheat a grill pan or frying pan and cook the chicken until tender, 3–4 minutes.

4. Dip your hands in cold water to prevent the rice from sticking, and take about 1 tablespoon of the sushi rice and squeeze it into an oblong shape. Take one strip of nori and wrap it around the rice oblong. Wet the ends of the nori and stick it together. The sides of the nori should come just slightly above the rice, so that you have a sort of container for the filling. Repeat with the remaining rice and nori strips.

5. Use a teaspoon to fill the tops of the "battleships" with the chicken. Arrange the battleship sushi pieces on a platter. Garnish half the battleships with a dab of chili sauce and sprinkle with chives. Garnish the remaining battleships with a dab of mayonnaise and 1–2 capers.

CORN battleship sushi

Serves 4 • Preparation 20 minutes + time for the rice
Difficulty 2

½	recipe sushi rice (see page 7)		storebought or home-made spicy mayonnaise see page 10)
3	nori sheets		
1	(6-ounce/180-g) corn kernels, drained	1	teaspoon soy sauce
3	tablespoons	2–3	teaspoons snipped fresh chives, to garnish

1. Prepare the sushi rice. Cut each nori sheet into six equal strips.

2. Dip your hands in cold water to prevent the rice from sticking and take about 1 tablespoon of the sushi rice and squeeze it into an oblong shape. Take a strip of nori and wrap it around the rice oblong. Wet the ends of the nori and stick it together. The sides of the nori should come just slightly above the rice, so that you have a sort of container for the filling. Repeat with the remaining rice and nori strips.

3. Mix the corn, mayonnaise, and soy sauce in a small bowl. Use a teaspoon to fill the tops of the "battleships." Garnish with chives and serve.

FISH ROE battleship sushi

Serves 4–6 • Preparation 20 minutes + time for the rice
Difficulty 2

1	recipe sushi rice (see page 7)	3	ounces (90 g) salmon roe
5	nori sheets	3	ounces (90 g) lumpfish roe
	Wasabi paste		Soy sauce, to serve
3	ounces (90 g) flying fish roe		

1. Prepare the sushi rice. Cut each nori sheet into six equal strips.

2. Dip your hands in cold water to prevent the rice from sticking and take about 1 tablespoon of the sushi rice and squeeze it into an oblong shape. Take a strip of nori and wrap it around the rice oblong. Wet the ends of the nori and stick it together. The sides of the nori should come just slightly above the rice, so that you have a sort of container for the filling. Repeat with the remaining rice and nori strips.

3. Use a teaspoon to fill the tops of the "battleships" with fish roe. Arrange the battleship sushi pieces on a platter. Serve with soy sauce.

SHRIMP SALAD battleship sushi

Serves 4–6 • Preparation 20 minutes + time for the rice
Cooking 3–4 minutes • Difficulty 2

1	recipe sushi rice (see page 7)		Salt
5	nori sheets	5	ounces (150 g) small, peeled cooked shrimp (prawns)
4	tablespoons frozen peas		
1	carrot, cut into tiny cubes	1	recipe spicy may-onnaise (see page 10)

1. Prepare the sushi rice. Cut each nori sheet into six equal strips.

2. Cook the peas and carrots in a small pot of lightly salted boiling water until just tender, 3–4 minutes. Drain well. Chop the shrimp coarsely and place in a small bowl. Add ⅓ cup of the spicy mayonnaise, and the peas and carrots. Mix well.

3. Dip your hands in cold water to prevent the rice from sticking and take about 1 tablespoon of the sushi rice and squeeze it into an oblong shape. Take a strip of nori and wrap it around the rice oblong. Wet the ends of the nori and stick it together. The sides of the nori should come just slightly above the rice, so that you have a sort of container for the filling. Repeat with the remaining rice and nori strips.

4. Use a teaspoon to fill the top of each battleship with some of the shrimp mixture.

SMOKED SALMON battleship sushi

Serves 4–6 • Preparation 20 minutes + time for the rice
Difficulty 2

1	recipe sushi rice (see page 7)		unwaxed lemon, cut in tiny v-shapes, to garnish
5	nori sheets		
5	ounces (150 g) smoked salmon		Long thin slices of cucumber, to garnish
1	recipe spicy may-onnaise (see page 10)		
	Paper-thin slices of		

1. Prepare the sushi rice. Cut each nori sheet into six equal strips.

2. Dip your hands in cold water to prevent the rice from sticking and take about 1 tablespoon of the sushi rice and squeeze it into an oblong shape. Take a strip of nori and wrap it around the rice oblong. Wet the ends of the nori and stick it together. The sides of the nori should come just slightly above the rice, so that you have a sort of container for the filling. Repeat with the remaining rice and nori strips.

3. Cut the smoked salmon into rectangles and fit one into the top of each battleship. Garnish each one with a dab of spicy mayonnaise, a piece of lemon, and a twist of cucumber.

These sushi balls are easy to make. If you are a novice sushi-maker, they are a really good place to begin.

VEGETARIAN sushi balls

Sushi Balls
1	recipe sushi rice (see page 7)
2	medium carrots, finely grated
6	scallions (spring onions), finely chopped
1/4	cup toasted white sesame seeds
1/4	cup toasted black sesame seeds

Wasabi Ginger Sauce
1	tablespoon wasabi powder
1/4	cup (60 ml) water
1	clove garlic
1	tablespoon peeled finely chopped fresh ginger
2	tablespoons peanut oil
3	tablespoons rice vinegar
1/3	cup (90 ml) soy sauce

Serves 4-6 • Preparation 20 minutes + time for the rice + 30 minutes to chill • Difficulty 1

Sushi Balls

1. Prepare the sushi rice and let cool.

2. Stir the carrots and scallions into the rice until well mixed.

3. Spread the white sesame seeds on one plate and the black sesame seeds on another plate.

4. Dip your hands in cold water to prevent the rice from sticking, and take 1-2 tablespoons of rice mixture and squeeze into a ball. Roll half the balls in the white sesame seeds and half in the black sesame seeds. Place on a serving platter and chill for 30 minutes.

Wasabi Ginger Sauce

1. Combine all the sauce ingredients in a bowl and mix well. Serve with the sushi balls.

If you liked this recipe, you will love these as well.

CALIFORNIA ROLL
sushi balls

UMEBOSHI PLUM
sushi balls

SMOKED SALMON
sushi balls

CHICORY BOATS with carpaccio

1   recipe sushi rice (see page 7)
    Wasabi paste
    About 16 medium chicory
    (witloof) leaves
    Wasabi paste
7   ounces (200 g) top-quanity
    steak (tenderloin is ideal),
    sliced about $1/8$ inch (3 mm)
    thick
2   nori sheets

72

Serves 4-6 • Preparation 20 minutes + time for the rice • Difficulty 1

1. Prepare the sushi rice. Set out the chicory leaves. Cut the
    nori sheets into strips about $1/2$ inch (1 cm) wide.

2. Cut the beef into rectangles that will fit over the chicory
    leaves.

3. Dip your hands in cold water to prevent the rice from
    sticking, and take a large handful of rice and press it into a
    long oblong that will fit into a chicory leaf. Place in the leaf
    and top with a dab or two of wasabi. Cover with a piece of
    beef. Wrap a strip of nori around the middle, sticking the
    ends together with a little water, and tucking them
    underneath the chicory leaf. Place on a platter and repeat
    with the remaining ingredients.

SMOKED SALMON & ASPARAGUS *nigiri*

1   recipe sushi rice (see page 7)
24   thin stalks asparagus, trimmed
7   ounces (200 g) sliced smoked
     salmon
2   nori sheets
     Wasabi paste

Serves 4–6 • Preparation 20 minutes + time for the rice • Cooking 1–2 minutes • Difficulty 1

1. Prepare the sushi rice. Cut the nori sheets into strips about $^1/_2$ inch (1 cm) wide.

2. Cook the asparagus in a saucepan of lightly salted boiling water until just crisp-tender, 1–2 minutes. Drain well.

3. Cut the salmon into pieces measuring about 2 inches (5 cm) square.

4. Dip your hands in cold water to prevent the rice from sticking, and take a handful of sushi rice and press it into an oblong. Dab the top of the rice with a little wasabi. Cover with two stalks of asparagus and top with a piece of salmon. Wrap a strip of nori around the middle, sticking the ends together with a little water underneath. Place on a platter and repeat with the remaining ingredients.

Sushi first became widely popular outside Japan in the 1960s when a number of Japanese sushi chefs set up shop in Los Angeles. The California sushi roll was invented at the Tokyo Kaikan restaurant by Ichiro Mashita and it quickly became a classic. There are many variations and derivations from the popular inside-out roll. This is probably the quickest and easiest of them all to prepare.

CALIFORNIA ROLL sushi balls

1	recipe sushi rice (see page 7)
1	avocado, peeled and pitted
2	teaspoons freshly squeezed lemon juice
	Wasabi paste
1	small carrot, finely shredded
$^1/_2$	cup finely chopped cucumber
3	ounces (90 g) sliced smoked salmon, chopped
2–3	tablespoons storebought or homemade pickled ginger (see page 9)
$^3/_4$	cup (120 g) toasted white sesame seeds
	Soy sauce, to serve

Serves 4–6 • Preparation 15 minutes + time for the rice + 1 hour to chill
Difficulty 1

1. Prepare the sushi rice.

2. Mash the avocado and lemon juice together in a bowl.

3. Dip your hands in cold water to prevent the rice from sticking, and divide the rice into 20 equal portions. Place one portion on a large square of plastic wrap (cling film). Using your fingertips, press the rice into a $^1/_4$-inch (5-mm) thick round. Dab with a little wasabi.

4. Spoon 2 teaspoons of avocado mixture into the center of the round. Top with 2–3 teaspoons each of carrot, cucumber, salmon, and pickled ginger. Using the plastic wrap, lift and fold the rice mixture around the filling to form a ball. Unwrap the ball and place on a platter. Repeat with the remaining ingredients.

5. Roll the sushi balls in the sesame seeds. Place on a serving platter. Cover and chill for 1 hour. Serve with soy sauce.

If you liked this recipe, you will love these as well.

RAINBOW
sushi rolls

CALIFORNIA
sushi rolls

VEGETARIAN
sushi balls

UMEBOSHI PLUM sushi balls

Serves 4–6 • Preparation 15 minutes • Cooking 15–20 minutes • Difficulty 2

3	cups (300 g) cooked brown rice		or other basil
3/4	cup (180 ml) soy sauce	8	umeboshi plums, pitted and puréed
3	tablespoons finely chopped fresh holy basil, Thai basil,	2	cups (500 ml) vegetable oil

1. Mix the cooked rice, basil, and 3 tablespoons of the soy sauce in a large bowl until the rice becomes sticky.

2. Dip your hands in cold water to prevent the rice from sticking and roll the rice mixture into egg-sized balls. Make a hollow in the center of each ball and add 1 teaspoon umeboshi purée. Close up the balls to seal in the filling.

3. Heat the oil in a deep-fryer or deep frying pan until very hot. Fry the balls in small batches for 4–5 minutes, until golden brown.

4. Drain well on paper towels. Serve hot with the remaining soy sauce for dipping.

SMOKED SALMON sushi balls

Serves 4–6 • Preparation 20 minutes + time for the rice Difficulty 2

1	recipe sushi rice (see page 7)	5	ounces (150 g) smoked salmon slices, cut into 1-inch (2.5-cm) squares (32 squares)
4	nori sheets, cut into 1-inch (2.5-cm) squares (32 squares)		Wasabi paste

1. Prepare the sushi rice.

2. Place 32 squares of plastic wrap (cling film) on a work surface. Place a nori square at the center of each one. Place a square of smoked salmon on top of the nori. Place a dab of wasabi on the salmon.

3. Dip your hands in cold water to prevent the rice from sticking and place 2 tablespoons of rice on the smoked salmon. Bring the edges of the plastic wrap up and twist to surround the rice and form it into a ball. Let rest in the plastic wrap in the refrigerator until just before serving.

MUSHROOM INARI sushi

Serves 4–6 • Preparation 20 minutes + time for the rice Cooking 3–4 minutes • Difficulty 2

1	recipe sushi rice (see page 7)	1/2	cup (125 ml) soy sauce
24	shiitake mushroom caps, thinly sliced	12	pre-packed inari wraps

1. Prepare the sushi rice.

2. Combine the mushrooms and 3 tablespoons of the soy sauce in a medium frying pan. Cook over medium heat for 3–4 minutes, until softened. Stir the mushroom and soy sauce mixture into the rice.

3. Tightly pack the inari pouches with the rice mixture and top each with a mushroom slice. Serve with the remaining soy sauce for dipping.

INARI sushi

Serves 4–6 • Preparation 20 minutes + time for the rice Difficulty 2

1/2	recipe sushi rice (see page 7)	1/2	cucumber, cut in batons
2	tablespoons black sesame seeds, toasted	1	carrot, cut into batons
12	pre-packed inari wraps		Soy sauce, to serve
			Pickled ginger to serve

1. Prepare the sushi rice.

2. Mix the sesame seeds into the rice. Press into twelve balls and place inside the inari wraps.

3. Serve the inari pouches with the vegetables and plenty of soy sauce and pickled ginger.

Sushi cones, known as *temaki* in Japanese, are the easiest type of sushi to prepare. Japanese hosts will often present their guests with sheets of nori and fresh ingredients laid out on a platter so that they can prepare their own. Always serve the cones as soon as possible after rolling, so the nori doesn't become soggy.

SMOKED SALMON & VEGGIE sushi cones

¹/₂	recipe sushi rice (see page 7)
5	nori sheets, cut in half
¹/₂	cup (120 ml) storebought or homemade spicy mayonnaise (see page 10)
7	ounces (200 g) smoked salmon, thinly sliced
1	red or yellow bell pepper (capsicum), seeded and cut into long thin strips
2	small avocados, peeled, pitted, and cut into long thin strips
2	medium carrots, shaved into long ribbons
1	small cucumber, with peel, seeds removed, cut into long thin strips
1	cup (50 g) baby spinach leaves
¹/₂	cup (120 ml) soy sauce, to serve
1	tablespoon wasabi, to serve
	Storebought or homemade pickled ginger (see page 9), to serve

Serves 4 • Preparation 20 minutes + time for the rice • Difficulty 1

1. Prepare the sushi rice.

2. Place a nori sheet shiny side down in one hand. Spread 3–4 tablespoons of sushi rice in a thin layer over one half of the nori sheet. Dab with some spicy mayonnaise. Cover with smoked salmon, bell pepper, avocado, carrot, cucumber, and spinach leaves, placing them diagonally across the rice.

3. Roll the nori around the filling to create a cone by folding the bottom left-hand corner of the nori sheet toward the top right-hand corner and rolling. Lightly moisten the corner of the nori sheet and press down to seal.

4. Repeat with the remaining ingredients to make 10 cones. Serve with the soy sauce, wasabi, and pickled ginger.

If you liked this recipe, you will love these as well.

VEGETARIAN
sushi cones

BROWN RICE & SHRIMP
sushi cones

TUNA & VEGGIE
sushi cones

BROWN RICE & SHRIMP sushi cones

1½ cups (300 g) brown rice

3 cups (750 ml) water

¼ cup (60 ml) rice vinegar

1 pound (500 g) large shrimp, cooked and peeled

½ cup (120 ml) spicy mayonnaise, storebought or homemade (see page 10)

5 nori sheets, cut in half

Wasabi paste

1 avocado, peeled, pitted, and cut into long thin strips

1 small cucumber, with peel, seeds removed, cut into long thin strips

2 tablespoons black sesame seeds

4 tablespoons flying fish roe

2 scallions (green onions), thinly sliced on the diagonal

Soy sauce, to serve

Storebought or homemade pickled ginger (see page 9), to serve

Serves 4–6 • Preparation 30 minutes + 1 hour to cool • Cooking 40–45 minutes • Difficulty 2

1. Combine the brown rice and cold water in a saucepan and bring to a boil. Cover and simmer over low heat until tender, 40–45 minutes. Drain and stir in the rice vinegar. Transfer to a colander and let cool.

2. Chop the shrimp coarsely and mix with the mayonnaise.

3. Place a nori sheet shiny side down in one hand. Spread 3–4 tablespoons of sushi rice in a thin layer over one half of the nori sheet. Dab with some wasabi. Top with some shrimp mix and any combination of the other ingredients.

4. Roll the nori around the filling to create a cone by folding the bottom left-hand corner of the nori sheet toward the top right-hand corner and rolling. Lightly moisten the corner of the nori sheet and press down to seal.

5. Repeat with the remaining ingredients to make ten cones. Serve with the soy sauce and pickled ginger.

TUNA & VEGGIE sushi cones

½	recipe sushi rice (see page 7)
20	green beans, trimmed
5	nori sheets, cut in half
½	cup (120 ml) spicy mayonnaise, storebought or homemade (see page 10)
6	ounces (180 g) sashimi-grade tuna, cut into thin strips
1	small jar grilled red bell peppers (capsicums), cut into long thin strips
2	small avocados, peeled, pitted and cut into thin strips
	Soy sauce, to serve
	Wasabi paste, to serve
	Storebought or homemade pickled ginger (see page 9), to serve

Serves 4 • Preparation 20 minutes + time for the rice • Cooking 2 minutes • Difficulty 1

1. Prepare the sushi rice.

2. Blanch the green beans in lightly salted boiling water for 2 minutes. Drain well.

3. Place a nori sheet shiny side down in one hand. Spread 3–4 tablespoons of sushi rice in a thin layer over one half of the nori sheet. Dab with a little spicy mayonnaise. Cover with strips of tuna, bell pepper, and avocado, placing them diagonally across the rice. Add two green beans.

4. Roll the nori around the filling to create a cone by folding the bottom left-hand corner of the nori sheet toward the top right-hand corner and rolling. Lightly moisten the corner of the nori sheet and press down to seal.

5. Repeat with the remaining ingredients to make 10 cones. Serve with the soy sauce, wasabi, and pickled ginger.

scattered sushi

TOKYO-STYLE scattered sushi

16	dried shiitake mushrooms
1	recipe sushi rice (see page 7)
1	cup (250 ml) dashi
1/2	cup (120 ml) dark soy sauce
1/4	cup (60 ml) mirin
4	tablespoons (60 ml) saké
2	tablespoons sugar
4	medium carrots, cut lengthwise into long strips
6	large shrimp (prawns)
6	pieces squid, about 3 inches (8 cm) square
12	ounces (350 g) sashimi-quality fresh raw tuna
2	large eggs + 4 large egg yolks
6	snow peas (mangetout), parboiled, and thinly sliced
	Kinome sprigs, to garnish
	Sesame seeds, to garnish
	Storebought or homemade pickled ginger (see page 9), to serve

Serves 6–8 • Preparation 45 minutes + time for the rice + 4 hours to soak • Cooking 25–30 minutes • Difficulty 2

1. Place the dried shiitake mushrooms in a bowl and cover with warm water. Let soak until softened, about 4 hours. Drain. Prepare the sushi rice.

2. Heat 1/2 cup (120 ml) of dashi with 1/4 cup (60 ml) of soy sauce, the mirin, and 2 tablespoons of saké in a small saucepan over medium heat. Add the mushrooms and simmer for 15 minutes. Remove from the heat and let rest in the liquid for 2 hours. Drain, and cut the best-looking twelve mushrooms in half and set aside. Chop the remaining mushrooms.

3. Heat the remaining dashi with the remaining soy sauce, remaining 2 tablespoons of saké, and the sugar in a small saucepan over medium heat. Add the carrots and simmer until just tender, 7–8 minutes. Drain and let cool.

4. Cook the shrimp in a pot of boiling water until pink, 2–3 minutes. Drain and let cool. Shell and devein. Slit in half lengthwise by cutting them open underneath.

5. Score the outside of the squid diagonally at intervals of about 1/4 inch (5 mm). Dip the pieces into boiling water for 20–30 seconds, until they curl. Plunge into ice water. Drain.

6. Cut the tuna against the grain into slices about 1/4 inch (5 mm) thick. Beat the eggs with the yolks and strain. Make a large thin omelet. When cool, fold and cut into thin strips.

7. Toss the sushi rice with the chopped mushrooms. Put the rice in a large serving platter. Scatter with the egg strips, mushroom halves, shrimp, squid, tuna, carrots, and snow peas. Garnish with sprigs of kinome and sesame seeds, and serve with the pickled ginger.

Scattered sushi, known in Japan as *chirashizushi*, consists of sushi rice with ingredients such as vegetables and fish scattered decoratively over the top. Sometimes some of the ingredients are mixed into the sushi rice, while the others are scattered on top. There are no hard and fast rules, so feel free to adapt the ingredients to your personal tastes or what you have on hand.

SPRING FESTIVAL scattered sushi

1   recipe sushi rice (see page 7)

Radish Petals
4   radishes, trimmed
2   tablespoons rice vinegar
2   tablespoons sugar

Egg Petals
1   large egg, beaten
    Salt
$^1/_2$ teaspoon cornstarch (cornflour), mixed with 1 teaspoon water
    Sunflower oil, for frying

Vegetables
6   dried shiitake mushrooms
5   tablespoons sugar
$2^1/_2$ tablespoons mirin
$^1/_4$ cup (60 ml) chicken stock
1   teaspoon soy sauce
1   small carrot, sliced into 1-inch (2.5-cm) matchsticks
8   snow peas (mangetout), trimmed
4   ounces (120 g) cod fillet
1   tablespoon saké
8   ounces (250 g) small shrimp (prawns), peeled and lightly cooked
3   tablespoons white sesame seeds, lightly toasted in a dry frying pan

Serves 4–6 • Preparation 15 minutes + time for the rice + 6–12 hours to marinate • Cooking 20–25 minutes • Difficulty 2

1. Prepare the sushi rice.

Radish Petals

1. Cut tiny wedges out of each radish, then slice crosswise to form 5–6 petal shapes. Put the vinegar and sugar in a bowl and stir until the sugar has dissolved. Add the radish slices and marinate for 6 hours, or overnight.

Egg Petals

1. Mix the egg in a bowl with a pinch of salt and the cornstarch mixture. Heat a small frying pan, brush with oil, add the egg mixture and cook until set. Using molds, cut out small flower shapes from the omelet.

Vegetables

1. Soak the shiitake in warm water for 4 hours. Drain, reserving the soaking liquid. Discard the stems and thinly slice the caps. Combine the shiitake, $^1/_3$ cup (90 ml) of soaking liquid, 2 tablespoons of sugar, and mirin in a pan over low heat and simmer until the liquid evaporates.

2. Put the chicken stock in a saucepan, add $^1/_2$ teaspoon of sugar, a pinch of salt, and the carrot. Bring to a boil then simmer until just soft, 2–3 minutes. Let cool in the liquid.

3. Blanch the snow peas in salted water. Slice diagonally. Simmer the cod in boiling water for 3–4 minutes, then drain. Return to a dry saucepan, add the saké, remaining sugar, and salt. Use a fork to finely flake over low heat.

4. Stir the shiitake, carrot, snow peas, fish, shrimp, and sesame seeds into the rice. Top with the radish and egg petals and serve.

SALMON & TUNA scattered sushi

1   recipe sushi rice (see page 7)
2   tablespoons toasted white sesame seeds
4   ounces (100 g) sashimi-grade fresh salmon, sliced
4   ounces (100 g) sashimi-grade fresh tuna, sliced
2   teaspoons flying fish roe
2   tablespoons wakame seaweed
1   tablespoon storebought or homemade pickled ginger (see page 9)
    Wasabi paste, to serve
    Soy sauce, to serve

Serves 4-6 • Preparation 15 minutes + time for the rice • Difficulty 1

1. Prepare the sushi rice. Stir the toasted sesame seeds into the cooled the rice.

2. Divide the rice evenly among four to six serving bowls. Arrange slices of salmon, tuna, flying fish roe, wakamae seaweed, and pickled ginger on top. Serve with some wasabi and soy sauce.

SALMON & SHIITAKE scattered sushi

1 recipe sushi rice (see page 7)
8 dried shiitake mushrooms
3 tablespoons soy sauce
1 tablespoon + 2 teaspoons sugar
1 teaspoon saké
3 large eggs
1 tablespoon vegetable oil
8 ounces (250 g) sashimi-grade fresh salmon slices
  Wasabi paste
1 small cucumber, julienned
3 ounces (90 g) imitation crab, shredded
3 tablespoons white sesame seeds

Serves 4–6 • Preparation 15 minutes + time for the rice + 4¼ hours to soak • Cooking 15–20 minutes • Difficulty 1

1. Prepare the sushi rice.

2. Soak the shiitake in warm water for 4 hours. Drain, reserving the soaking liquid. Discard the stems and thinly slice the caps. Heat $^{2}/_{3}$ cup (150 ml) of the soaking water in a medium pan. Add the shiitake, 1 tablespoon soy sauce, 1 tablespoon sugar, and saké. Simmer on low heat until the liquid is almost gone. Set aside.

3. Whisk the eggs in a bowl with 2 teaspoons of sugar. Heat the oil in a large frying pan and pour in the egg mixture, swirling to make a thin omelet. Cut into thin strips.

4. Put the salmon in a bowl with the remaining soy sauce and a dab of wasabi. Marinate for 15 minutes, then drain.

5. Put the sushi rice on a large platter. Scatter with the shiitake, cucumber, crab meat, and omelet strips. Put the salmon on top. Sprinkle with the sesame seeds and serve.

Asparagus and salmon go very well together in this version of scattered sushi. However, if they are not in season, replace with flowering broccoli or mangetout.

SCATTERED SUSHI with shrimp & salmon roe

1	recipe sushi rice (see page 7)
5	dried shiitake mushrooms
2	teaspoons soy sauce
2	teaspoons mirin
2	teaspoons sugar + extra
2	teaspoons saké
2	carrots
	Salt
5	large eggs
1–2	tablespoons sesame oil
24	thin asparagus stalks
2	tablespoons white sesame seeds
20	large cooked shrimp (prawns), shelled and deveined
4	tablespoons salmon roe

Serves 4–6 • Preparation 15 minutes + time for the rice + 4 hours to soak • Cooking 20 minutes • Difficulty 2

1. Prepare the sushi rice.

2. Soak the shiitake mushrooms in warm water for 4 hours. Drain, reserving the liquid. Cut into $1/4$-inch (5-mm) strips. Simmer the shiitake strips in the reserved liquid, soy sauce, mirin, sugar, and 1 teaspoon of saké for about 10 minutes.

3. Cut the carrot lengthwise into thin sheets. Cut the sheets into $1/4$ x $1/2$-inch (5 x 10-mm) pieces. Simmer for 2 minutes in a little water with the remaining sake and salt.

4. Beat the eggs with a pinch of salt and sugar. Coat a hot frying pan with oil, and pour in half the mixture, swirling to create a very thin omelet. Turn the heat down, cover the pan, and turn the heat off; the omelet should be soft, and just set. Turn out onto a cutting board and let cool. Cut the omelet in half, and fold several times. Cut into thin strips. Repeat with the remaining egg mixture.

5. Parboil the asparagus in boiling water until bright green and just tender. Drain in a colander. Pour cold water over the asparagus to stop the cooking process. Drain, and cut on the diagonal into $1/4$-inch (5-mm) pieces.

6. Stir the sesame seeds into the sushi rice. Transfer to a large shallow serving bowl or sushi platter. Scatter the shiitake, carrot, and asparagus evenly over the rice. Top with the egg strips and finish with the shrimp and salmon roe.

RICH scattered sushi

1   recipe sushi rice (see page 7)
6   dried shiitake mushrooms, stalks discarded
1/2 large carrot, finely chopped
1/2 cup (120 ml) water
2   tablespoons sugar
     Salt
6   snow peas (mangetout), trimmed, thinly sliced diagonally
1   ounce (30 g) kanpyo (dried gourd shavings), rinsed
1 1/2 tablespoons soy sauce
5   ounces (150 g) whole peeled bamboo shoot, cut into short pieces
8   large eggs
1 1/2 teaspoons instant dashi stock granules
1   tablespoon mirin
1   tablespoon vegetable oil
12   ounces (350 g) sashimi-grade salmon, cut into 1 1/2-inch (4-cm) thick slices

Serves 4–6 • Preparation 20 minutes + time for the rice + 4 hours to soak • Cooking 35 minutes • Difficulty 2

1. Prepare the sushi rice. Soak the shiitake mushrooms in 2 cups (500 ml) of warm water for 4 hours. Drain and finely chop, reserving the soaking liquid.

2. Cook the carrot in the water with a pinch of sugar and salt over medium heat until soft, 3–4 minutes. Drain and let cool. Blanch the snow peas in boiling water. Drain.

3. Put the kanpyo in a sieve and rinse under cold running water. Rub 1 teaspoon of salt into the kanpyo and rinse again. Cook in a pan of boiling water until soft, about 5 minutes. Drain, then finely chop.

4. Place the reserved shiitake liquid, shiitakes, remaining sugar, soy sauce, kanpyo, and bamboo in a saucepan. Simmer for 20 minutes, until the water has almost evaporated. Let cool.

5. Whisk the eggs, dashi, and mirin in a bowl. Heat the oil in a small frying pan over low heat. Working in batches, pour in 1/4 cup of egg mixture at a time to make thin omelets. Cut into thin strips.

6. Stir the carrot and shiitake mixture into the rice. Put the rice mixture in a large serving bowl. Top with the salmon, snow peas, and omelet, and serve.

VEGETARIAN scattered sushi

1	recipe sushi rice (see page 7)
5	dried shiitake mushrooms
2	tablespoons saké
1	tablespoon mirin
2	teaspoons soy sauce
2	teaspoons sugar
2	carrots
	Salt
24	snow peas (mangetout), trimmed, thinly sliced diagonally
5	large eggs
1	tablespoon vegetable oil
2	tablespoons beni shoga (red julienned ginger)
2	tablespoons white sesame seeds

Serves 4–6 • Preparation 20 minutes + time for the rice + 4 hours to soak • Cooking 30 minutes • Difficulty 2

1. Prepare the sushi rice. Soak the shiitake mushrooms in 2 cups (500 ml) of warm water for 4 hours. Drain and cut into $1/4$-inch (5-mm) strips. Simmer in the reserved liquid, with 1 tablespoon of saké, the mirin, soy sauce, and sugar for 20 minutes.

2. Shave the carrot very thinly lengthwise. Cut into small pieces. Simmer in boiling water with the remaining sake and a pinch of salt for 2–3 minutes. Blanch the snow peas in boiling water. Drain.

3. Whisk the eggs with a pinch of salt and sugar. Heat the oil in a large frying pan and pour in half the mixture, swirling the egg to make a very thin omelet. Cut into thin strips. Repeat with the remaining egg mixture.

4. Stir the sesame seeds into the rice. Put the rice mixture in a large serving bowl. Top with the shiitake, carrots, snow peas, beni shoga, and omelet, and serve.

You can vary the ingredients in this colorful sushi, depending on what you like and have in the larder.

RAINBOW scattered sushi

1 recipe sushi rice (see page 7)
Mushrooms
8-10 dried shiitake mushrooms
$1/4$ cup (60 ml) shiitake stock (from soaking)
2 tablespoons soy sauce
1 tablespoon mirin
1 tablespoon honey
Carrots
2 medium carrots, cut into matchsticks
$1/2$ cup (120 ml) shiitake stock (from soaking)
2 tablespoons soy sauce
1 tablespoon mirin
1 tablespoon sugar
Peas
1 cup (150 g) frozen peas
$1/2$ cup (120 ml) boiling water
$1/2$ teaspoon salt
1 tablespoon honey
Tofu
8 ounces (250 g) firm tofu, cut into matchsticks
1 tablespoon soy sauce
2 tablespoons honey
$1/2$ teaspoon salt
Nori
3-4 nori sheets

Serves 4-6 • Preparation 20 minutes + time for the rice + 4 hours to soak • Cooking 20 minutes • Difficulty 2

1. Prepare the sushi rice.

Mushrooms

1. Soak the mushrooms in cold water for 4 hours. Drain, reserving the soaking liquid. Slice the mushrooms thinly.

2. Combine the mushrooms, $1/4$ cup (60 ml) of the reserved soaking liquid, soy sauce, mirin, and honey in a small pan and simmer over low heat 15 minutes. Drain.

Carrots

1. Combine the carrots, $1/2$ cup (120 ml) of the reserved soaking liquid, soy sauce, mirin, and sugar in a pan over medium heat and cook until tender, 3-4 minutes. Drain.

Peas

1. Cook the peas in the boiling water with the salt and honey until just tender 2-3 minutes.

Tofu

1. Heat all the ingredients in a frying pan over medium heat until the tofu absorbs the flavors and turns yellow.

Nori

1. Pass each nori sheet over an open gas flame or electric burner until crisp. With a pair of scissors, cut each sheet in half, then stack the sheets together. Shred with the scissors.

To Serve

1. Divide the rice evenly among four to six serving plates. Arrange the mushrooms, carrots, peas, tofu, and nori on top of the rice in separate piles. Serve.

EASY scattered sushi

1	recipe sushi rice (see page 7)
2	cups (300 g) frozen green peas
	Handful green beans, sliced into short pieces
	Handful snow peas (mangetout), sliced into short pieces
1	small yellow summer squash, thinly sliced
3	large eggs
	Salt
	Sugar
1	tablespoons peanut oil
1	medium carrot, grated
1	small cucumber, peeled, seeded, grated
2	scallions (spring onions), thinly sliced
4	tablespoons pickled ginger
3	tablespoons sesame seeds, lightly toasted

Serves 4–6 • Preparation 15 minutes + time for the rice • Cooking 5 minutes • Difficulty 1

1. Prepare the sushi rice.

2. Combine the peas, green beans, snow peas, and summer squash in a steamer and steam until just tender, about 5 minutes.

3. Whisk the eggs with a pinch of salt and sugar. Heat the oil in a large frying pan and pour in the egg mixture, swirling to make a thin omelet. Coarsely chop the omelet.

4. Add the omelet and all the other ingredients to the rice and mix gently. Transfer to a serving bowl, and serve warm or at room temperature.

SALMON & AVOCADO scattered sushi

1   recipe sushi rice (see page 7)
1   cucumber
1   stalk celery
6   ounces (180 g) smoked salmon
2   avocados, peeled and pitted
4   tablespoons flying fish roe
1   recipe citrus dipping sauce (ponzu), for serving (see page 10)

Serves 4–6 • Preparation 15 minutes + time for the rice • Difficulty 1

1. Prepare the sushi rice.

2. Cut the cucumber and celery into small cubes. Cut the smoked salmon and avocado into bite-sized pieces.

3. Stir the cucumber and celery cubes into the rice, mixing well. Divide evenly among four to six serving plates. Arrange the avocado cubes and salmon pieces on top. Top with teaspoons of flying fish roe and serve with the citrus dipping sauce.

If liked, replace the tuna with another type of fish. Since it is served raw, be sure to choose very fresh, high-quality fish (as you would for sashimi).

96

TUNA & SHIITAKE scattered sushi

8 dried shiitake mushrooms
1 recipe sushi rice (see page 7)
8 ounces (250 g) sashimi-grade fresh tuna slices
3 tablespoons soy sauce
  Wasabi paste
1½ tablespoons sugar
1 teaspoon mirin
4 large eggs
1 tablespoon sesame oil
1 cucumber, julienned
2 ounces (60 g) imitation crab, shredded
4 tablespoons white sesame seeds
  Storebought or homemade pickled ginger (see page 9), to serve

Serves 4-6 • Preparation 20 minutes + time for the rice + 4 hours to soak • Cooking 5-10 minutes • Difficulty 2

1. Soak the shiitake mushrooms in 2 cups (500 ml) warm water for 4 hours. Reserve the soaking water.

2. Prepare the sushi rice. Marinate the tuna in 2 tablespoons of soy sauce and a dab of wasabi for 15 minutes.

3. Remove the stems from the shiitake and cut in half. Heat ⅔ cup (150 ml) of the soaking water in a medium pan. Add the shiitake and remaining soy sauce, 1 tablespoon of sugar, and the mirin. Simmer over low heat until the liquid is almost evaporated. Set aside.

4. Whisk the eggs in a bowl with the remaining sugar. Heat the oil in a large frying pan and pour in the egg mixture, swirling to make a thin omelet. Cut into thin strips.

5. Divide the rice evenly among four to six bowls. Cover with the mushrooms, cucumber, crab, omelet, and tuna. Sprinkle with sesame seeds. Serve with the pickled ginger.

If you liked this recipe, you will love these as well.

TOKYO-STYLE scattered sushi

SPRING FESTIVAL scattered sushi

SCATTERED SUSHI with shrimp & salmon roe

SEARED SQUID with sushi rice salad

1	recipe sushi rice (see page 7)

Dressing

	Handful of fresh mint, parsley, and cilantro (coriander)
1	(2-inch/5-cm) piece ginger, finely chopped
1	clove garlic, chopped
1	lime, juice only
1	tablespoon light soy sauce
1	tablespoon honey
3	tablespoons sunflower oil

Squid

2	large squid, cleaned, and sliced into rings
2	tablespoons storebought or homemade sweet chili sauce (see page 10)
1	tablespoon sunflower oil
	Salt and freshly ground black pepper

Salad

1	small cucumber, thinly diced
4	scallions (spring onions), thinly sliced diagonally
1	red chili, seeded and very finely sliced
2	tablespoons storebought or homemade pickled ginger (see page 9), finely chopped

Serves 4–6 • Preparation 15 minutes + time for the rice • Cooking 2 minutes • Difficulty 1

1. Prepare the sushi rice.

Dressing

1. Put all the dressing ingredients in a food processor and chop until almost smooth. Add the sunflower oil and chop until smooth. Chill until needed.

Squid

1. Heat a grill pan or wok over high heat. Mix the chili sauce and oil, brush over the squid, and season generously with salt and pepper. Sear the squid for 1 minute on each side.

Salad

1. Toss all the salad ingredients together in a bowl.

2. To serve, divide the rice evenly among four to six plates, top each with some salad and squid. Finish with a drizzle of the dressing and serve.

SEARED SALMON with sushi rice salad

1	recipe sushi rice (see page 7)
1	pound (500 g) salmon fillets, skinned
1	(2-inch/5-cm) piece ginger, finely chopped
2	cloves garlic, finely chopped
1	scallion (spring onion), finely chopped
1	tablespoon coriander seeds, crushed
	Salt and freshly ground black pepper
4	tablespoons (60 ml) saké
1	small pineapple
1	tablespoon butter
1	tablespoon red pepper flakes
1	avocado, peeled, pitted, and diced
1	small cucumber, diced
1	large tomato, diced
1	small bunch cilantro (coriander), chopped

Serves 6–8 • Preparation 25 minutes + time for the rice + 1 hour to marinate • Cooking 5–10 minutes • Difficulty 1

1. Prepare the sushi rice.

2. Combine the salmon, ginger, garlic, scallion, coriander, salt, and pepper in a bowl. Drizzle with saké and let stand for 1 hour. Peel the pineapple and dice the flesh. Set aside.

3. Melt the butter in a medium pan until bubbling. Add the red pepper flakes, pineapple, and 2 tablespoons of the saké marinade. Cook down until all the liquid has evaporated.

4. Heat a grill pan (griddle) or wok over high heat. Sear the salmon in the pan for 1–2 minutes. Remove from the pan and reserve.

5. Stir the avocado, cucumber, tomato, and cilantro into the sushi rice. Divide the rice salad evenly among six to eight serving plates. Slice the salmon and place on top of the rice. Spoon the pineapple mixture over the top and serve immediately.

SASHIMI platter

Mackerel

8	ounces (250 g) sashimi-grade fresh mackerel fillets, with skin
$1/2$	cup (100 g) coarse sea salt
$1/2$	cup (120 ml) rice vinegar
2	tablespoons water
$1/2$	tablespoons sugar
$1/2$	tablespoons mirin

Sea Bream

8	ounces (250 g) sashimi-grade fresh sea bream fillets, skin and bones removed
2-3	paper-thin slices unwaxed lemon

Tuna

8	ounces (250 g) sashimi-grade fresh tuna, skin and bones removed

Salmon

8	ounces (250 g) sashimi-grade fresh salmon, skin and bones removed

To Serve

	Perilla leaves, to garnish
	Shredded daikon, to garnish
	Wasabi paste, to serve
1-2	little bowls with sashimi sauces (see recipes on page 106)

Serves 6–8 • Preparation 20 minutes + 4–5 hours to drain & marinate
Difficulty 2

Mackerel

1. Lay the mackerel fillets in a large shallow bowl and sprinkle with the salt. Carefully rub the fillets with the salt. Transfer to a colander and let drain for 3–4 hours. Rinse carefully to remove excess salt and dry with a clean kitchen towel.

2. Mix the rice vinegar, water, sugar, and mirin in a large bowl, stirring until the sugar is dissolved. Add the mackerel and let marinate for 1 hour. The flesh will whiten. Remove the fillets from the marinade and carefully remove the thin outer skin. Leave the iridescent underskin on the fish.

3. Transfer the mackerel to a chopping board. Run your fingertips light over the fish, feeling for bones. Remove any bones. Cut the fillets into pieces about $1/4$ inch (5 mm) thick. Arrange on a platter.

Sea Bream

1. Lay the sea bream fillets on a chopping board and run your fingertips over it to check for bones. Remove any bones with tweezers. Arrange on the platter with the slices of lemon on top.

Tuna

1. Cut the tuna into pieces about $1/4$ inch (5 mm) thick and 2 inches (5 cm) long. Arrange on the platter.

Salmon

1. Cut the salmon into pieces about $1/4$ inch (5 mm) thick and 2 inches (5 cm) long. Arrange on the platter. Garnish the platter with the perilla leaves, daikon, and wasabi and serve with one or two sashimi sauces.

Red snapper is one of the best firm, white-fleshed fish you can buy. Its delicately flavored, pale pink flesh is perfect for sashimi, and for most other cooking techniques as well. As usual for sashimi, you will need to buy the freshest possible fish you can find. If fresh sashimi-grade red snapper is not available, you may replace it in this recipe with porgy, sea bass, or sea bream.

RED SNAPPER sashimi

1	pound (500 g) sashimi-grade fresh red snapper fillets, skin and bones removed
3	cloves garlic, very finely chopped
1	(2-inch/5-cm) piece fresh ginger, peeled and finely grated
2	tablespoons white sesame seeds, toasted
12	fresh chives
1/2	cup (120 ml) mustard & miso sauce (see page 106)

Serves 4 • Preparation 15 minutes • Difficulty 1

1. Cut the snapper into paper-thin slices. Arrange the slices on a serving platter. Dab each slice with some garlic and ginger. Sprinkle with the sesame seeds and chives.

2. Drizzle each portion with 1 tablespoon of the mustard & miso sauce. Serve with the rest of the sauce for dipping.

If you liked this recipe, you will love these as well.

SASHIMI platter

SPICY YELLOWTAIL sashimi

SEARED TUNA sashimi

SPICY YELLOWTAIL sashimi

12 ounces (350 g) sashimi-grade fresh yellowtail fillets, skin and bones removed

1 clove garlic, very finely chopped or minced

1 (1-inch/2.5-cm) piece peeled fresh ginger, cut in very fine julienne

2 scallions (spring onions), white and pale green parts only, thinly sliced

1 red jalapeno chili, seeded and finely diced

1 green jalapeno chili, seeded and finely diced

1 tablespoon soy sauce

1 tablespoon yuzu or grapefruit juice

2 tablespoons citrus dipping sauce (see page 10)

2 tablespoons extra-virgin olive oil

Lemon wedges, to garnish

Daikon radish, cut into julienne, to garnish

Serves 4 • Preparation 20 minutes • Cooking 30 seconds • Difficulty 2

1. Slice the yellowtail very thinly and arrange decoratively on a serving platter.

2. Sprinkle the garlic, ginger, scallions, and jalapeno evenly over the fish. Drizzle the soy sauce, yuzu juice, and citrus dipping sauce evenly over the fish.

3. Heat a small saucepan over high heat. Carefully add the oil to the hot pan and heat until it just begins to smoke, about 30 seconds. Remove from the heat and carefully pour over the fish. The hot oil will sear the outside of the fish.

4. Garnish with the lemon wedges and daikon and serve.

YELLOWTAIL & LEMON sashimi

1 pound (500 g) very fresh, premium yellowtail fillets, skin and bones removed

2 unwaxed lemons

4 scallions (green onions), pale green and white parts only, thinly sliced

Carrot curls, to garnish

Storebought or homemade tosa soy sauce (see page 106), to serve

Serves 4–6 • Preparation 20 minutes • Difficulty 2

1. Slice the yellowtail into paper-thin slices. Cut the lemons in half and remove the seeds. Slice into paper-thin slices.

2. Arrange half-moon slices of lemon around the edges of each serving plate. Partially cover the lemons with slices of yellowtail carefully rolled to fit.

3. Pile with the scallions and carrot curls in the center of the plates. Serve with the tosa soy sauce.

TOSA soy sauce

Makes about 1 cup (250 ml) • Preparation 10 minutes
+ 24 hours to marinate + 1 month to mature • Cooking
1–2 minutes • Difficulty 1

2	tablespoons mirin	1	cup (250 ml) dark soy sauce
5	teaspoons of saké		Handfuls of dried bonito flakes
1	(2-inch/5-cm) square dried kombu, wiped		

1. Heat the mirin and saké in a small saucepan until it produces fumes, then light the fumes with a long-handled match to burn off the alcohol.

2. Combine all the other ingredients in a bowl and let marinate in the refrigerator for 24 hours.

3. Strain the liquid into a jar, cover, and store in a dark cool place for at least 1 month to mature. Serve with sashimi.

MUSTARD & MISO sauce

Makes about 1 cup (250 ml) • Preparation 15 minutes
Difficulty 1

2	large egg yolks	1/2	cup (120 ml) + 2 tablespoons water
3/4	cup (200 g) white miso	3	tablespoons powder mustard
2	tablespoons saké	3	tablespoons rice vinegar
2	tablespoons dark brown sugar		

1. Place the egg yolks in a small bowl and whisk well. Add the miso, saké, and brown sugar and whisk again. Whisk in 1/2 cup (120 ml) of water.

2. Place in a double boiler over barely simmering water and stir until thickened. Remove from the heat and let cool to room temperature. Cover and chill until needed.

3. Just before serving, blend the mustard powder with the remaining 2 tablespoons of water. Stir in the rice vinegar, and serve with sashimi.

SESAME soy sauce

Serves 4 • Preparation 15 minutes • Cooking 1–2 minutes •
Difficulty 1

3	tablespoons white sesame seeds
1	tablespoon mirin
1/2	cup (120 ml) dark soy sauce

1. Dry-fry the sesame seeds in a frying pan over medium heat until golden brown. Grind to a paste with a mortar and pestle.

2. Heat the mirin in a small saucepan over medium heat until the alcohol is burnt off. You should have 1/2 tablespoon.

3. Stir the sesame paste and mirin into the soy sauce and serve with sashimi.

PLUM soy sauce

Makes about 1 cup (250 ml) • Preparation 10 minutes
Difficulty 2

4	whole red pickled plums (umeboshi)
1/2	cup (120 ml) dark soy sauce

1. Press the pickled plums through a sieve. Combine the sieved plum with the soy sauce, mixing well.

2. Serve with sashimi.

Deep red bluefin tuna is relatively fatty and the best-quality tuna on the market. Tender and flavorful, it lends itself perfectly to sashimi dishes. In this recipe, it is seared very quickly so that the edges are just barely cooked.

SEARED TUNA sashimi salad

Tuna

7	ounces (200 g) sashimi-grade fresh bluefin tuna fillet, in 1 piece
	Salt and freshly ground black pepper
1	tablespoon grapeseed oil

Salad

1	cucumber
2	baby daikon
$1/2$	endive (chicory)
$1/2$	red endive (treviso)
1	celery stalk
2	radishes
1	asparagus spear
1	carrot
2	myoga ginger (ginger bud)
2	ounces (60 g) lotus root
	Watercress

Dressing

1	small white onion, very finely chopped
4	tablespoons soy sauce
2	tablespoons rice vinegar
1	teaspoon sugar
$1/2$	teaspoon Japanese-style mustard powder
1	tablespoon water
	Salt and freshly ground black pepper
2	tablespoons grapeseed oil
2	tablespoons sesame oil

Serves 4 • Preparation 20 minutes • Cooking 1–2 minutes • Difficulty 2

Tuna

1. Season the tuna with salt and pepper. Heat the oil in a grill pan over high heat. Sear both sides of the tuna. When the surface has just started to cook and appears marbled, plunge the fillet into iced water, then pat with paper towels until completely dry.

Salad

1. Shave the vegetables very thinly with a vegetable peeler and place in a bowl of ice water for 5 minutes. Drain well. Toss the vegetables, then make a heap in the center of a serving plate.

2. Cut the tuna fillet into slices about $1/8$ inch (3 mm) thick and roll each slice into a cylinder. Arrange the tuna rolls around the vegetables. Garnish with the watercress.

Dressing

1. Rinse the onion in cold water to lessen its sharp flavor. Drain well.

2. Whisk the onion, soy sauce, vinegar, sugar, mustard powder, water, salt, and black pepper in a bowl.

3. When the salt has dissolved, add the grapeseed and sesame oils a little at a time, blending well.

4. Drizzle the dressing over the salad and serve.

SALMON sashimi salad

Sashimi Salad

8 ounces (250 g) sashimi-grade fresh wild salmon

½ small daikon, about 5 ounces (150 g), peeled

1 large carrot

4 scallions (green onions), pale green and white parts only

1 tablespoon storebought or homemade pickled ginger (see page 9)

3 teaspoons toasted sesame seeds

Dressing

2 tablespoons soy sauce

2 tablespoons mirin

1 tablespoon rice vinegar

1 tablespoon vegetable oil

1 teaspoon sesame oil

1 teaspoon castor sugar

Serves 4-6 • Preparation 20 minutes • Difficulty 2

Sashimi Salad

1. Thinly slice the salmon into strips about 1 x 2 inches (2.5 x 5 cm) long. Cut the daikon, carrot, scallions, and pickled ginger into thin matchsticks.

2. Place the salmon and vegetables in a bowl.

Dressing

1. Whisk the soy sauce, mirin, rice vinegar, oils, and sugar in a small bowl. Add to the salad and toss gently.

2. Divide the salad evenly among serving dishes. Sprinkle with the sesame seeds and serve.

SALMON & GINGER sashimi

¼ cup (60 ml) + 2 tablespoons soy sauce

1 teaspoon freshly squeezed lime juice

1 teaspoon freshly squeezed orange juice

8 ounces (250 g) sashimi-grade fresh wild salmon, cut in ¼-inch (5-mm) thick slices

One ¼-inch (5-mm) piece fresh ginger, sliced paper-thin and cut into thin matchsticks (about 24 pieces)

1 tablespoon snipped fresh chives

2 tablespoons grapeseed oil

1 teaspoon Asian sesame oil

2 teaspoons roasted sesame seeds

2 tablespoons fresh cilantro (coriander) leaves

Serves 4 • Preparation 15 minutes • Cooking 2 minutes • Difficulty 2

1. Mix 2 tablespoons of soy sauce with the lime and orange juices in a small bowl.

2. Toss the salmon with the remaining ¼ cup (60 ml) of soy sauce and let stand for 1 minute, then drain. Divided the slices of salmon evenly among four serving plates and top with the ginger and chives.

3. Heat the grapeseed and sesame oils in a small saucepan over medium heat until smoking, about 2 minutes. Drizzle the hot oil over the salmon pieces. Spoon the soy and citrus sauce over the top. Sprinkle with the sesame seeds and cilantro leaves and serve.

Mackerel is a tasty, firm, and inexpensive fish that is available all year round. It is best when really fresh; you can tell how fresh it is by looking at its skin, which should be vivid and colorful.

MACKEREL sashimi salad

Sashimi Salad

1	pound (500 g) mackerel fillets
1/2	cup (100 g) coarse sea salt
1	cup (250 ml) Japanese rice wine vinegar
1/4	cup (60 ml) water
1	tablespoon sugar
1	tablespoon mirin
5	ounces (150 g) edamame (soy) beans
4	cups (200 g) baby salad leaves
1	pink grapefruit
2	tablespoons white sesame seeds, toasted

Dressing

2	tablespoons freshly squeezed lime juice
1	teaspoon wasabi
1	teaspoon sweet chili sauce (see page 10)
1/2	cup (120 ml) mild extra-virgin olive oil

Serves 6 • Preparation 20 minutes + 4–5 hours to drain & marinate
Cooking 2 minutes • Difficulty 2

Sashimi Salad

1. Lay the mackerel fillets in a large shallow bowl and sprinkle with the salt. Carefully rub the fillets with the salt. Transfer to a colander and let drain for 3–4 hours. Rinse carefully to remove excess salt and dry with a clean kitchen towel.

2. Mix the rice vinegar, water, sugar, and mirin in a large plastic bowl, stirring until the sugar has dissolved. Add the mackerel and let marinate for 1 hour. The flesh will have whitened. Remove the fillets from the marinade and carefully remove the thin outer skin from the fish. Leave the iridescent underskin on the fish.

3. Transfer the fillets to a chopping board. Run your fingertips light over the fish, feeling for bones. Remove any bones using tweezers. Cut the mackerel into small cubes.

4. Blanch the edamame beans in boiling water for 2 minutes. Drain and let cool.

5. Place the salad leaves in a bowl. Peel the grapefruit and divide into segments. Cut each segment in half. Toss over the leaves. Top with the edamame beans and mackerel. Sprinkle with the sesame seeds.

Dressing

1. Whisk the lime juice, wasabi, sweet chili sauce, and oil together until well mixed. Season with salt and pepper. Drizzle over the salad and serve.

miso soups

SHRIMP & UDON NOODLE miso soup

12	ounces (350 g) dried udon noodles
24	(about 1 pound/500 g) small cooked shrimp (prawns), peeled, heads removed
5	ounces (150 g) silken firm tofu, cut into small squares
8	cups (2 liters) water
$^3/_4$	cup (200 g) white miso paste
1	tablespoon finely grated fresh ginger
2	tablespoons soy sauce
1	bunch asparagus, trimmed, cut into lengths diagonally
12	ounces (350 g) mixed Asian mushrooms (oyster, shimeji, shiitake, etc)
2	cups (100 g) baby spinach leaves
2	scallions (spring onions), trimmed, thinly sliced diagonally

Serves 6–8 • Preparation 10 minutes • Cooking 10–15 minutes
Difficulty 1

1. Cook the noodles in a large saucepan of boiling water until just tender, about 8 minutes, or according to the instructions on the package. Drain well. Divide the noodles evenly among six to eight serving bowls. Top each bowl with some shrimp and tofu.

2. Put the water and miso paste in a medium saucepan over medium-high heat. Bring to a boil, whisking often, until the miso dissolves.

3. Reduce the heat to low. Add the ginger and soy sauce and simmer for 2 minutes. Add the asparagus, mushrooms, and spinach, and simmer for 30 seconds, until the spinach is just wilted.

4. Ladle the soup into the bowls over the noodles. Sprinkle with the scallions and serve hot.

If you liked this recipe, you will love these as well.

SOBA NOODLE
miso soup

FENNEL
miso soup

ENOKI MUSHROOM
& SCALLION miso soup

SOBA NOODLE miso soup

Serves 4 • Preparation 10 minutes + 30 minutes to soak
Cooking 15-20 minutes • Difficulty 1

1/2	ounce (15 g) dried shiitake mushrooms	2	tablespoons red miso paste
1 1/2	cups (375 ml) boiling water	3	tablespoons white miso paste
8	ounces (250 g) dried soba noodles	3	scallions (spring onions), thinly sliced diagonally
8	cups (2 liters) water	4	ounces (120 g) button mushrooms, sliced
1	(1-inch/2.5-cm) piece fresh ginger, peeled and thinly sliced		

1. Soak the shiitake mushrooms in the boiling water for 30 minutes. Drain, reserving the liquid. Thinly slice the mushrooms. Cook the noodles in a large pan of boiling water until tender, 4-5 minutes. Drain.

2. Place the water, ginger, and reserved soaking liquid in a saucepan over high heat. Bring to a boil, then decrease the heat to low. Add both miso pastes and whisk until combined. Add the scallions, shiitake, and button mushrooms, and stir until well combined.

3. Divide the noodles and soup evenly among four serving bowls. Serve hot.

TOFU NOODLE miso soup

Serves 4 • Preparation 15 minutes • Difficulty 1

6	cups (1.5 liters) boiling water	1	bunch asparagus, trimmed, thinly sliced diagonally
2	tablespoons white miso paste	12	ounces (350 g) silken tofu, cut into small squares
12	ounces (350 g) dried udon noodles	1/4	cup snipped fresh chives
2	carrots, peeled, cut into matchsticks		
2	scallions (spring onions), thinly sliced		

1. Put the water in a large saucepan over medium heat. Add the miso and stir to combine. Decrease the heat to low. Add the noodles and gently stir to separate. Add the carrot, scallions, and asparagus, and cook until the asparagus is bright green and just tender, 1-2 minutes.

2. Divide the noodles and soup evenly among four serving bowls. Top with the tofu and sprinkle with the chives. Serve hot.

FENNEL miso soup

Serves 6 • Preparation 20 minutes • Cooking 35-45 minutes • Difficulty 2

2	tablespoons vegetable oil	1	small red chili, sliced
1	pound (500 g) fennel bulbs, finely sliced	1	teaspoon fennel seeds
1	carrot, julienned		Salt
	Whites of 2 leeks, sliced	3	tablespoons barley miso
2	potatoes, peeled and diced	6	cups (1.5 liters) water
1	(1-inch/2.5-cm) piece fresh ginger, peeled and finely chopped	3	cups (150 g) watercress, chopped + extra to garnish
1	clove garlic, finely chopped	5	snow peas (mangetout), halved
1/2	small green chili, sliced	1	tablespoon freshly squeezed lemon juice

1. Heat the oil in a large soup pot over medium heat. Add the fennel, carrot, leeks, and potatoes and sauté until the vegetables are softened, 8-10 minutes. Stir in the ginger, garlic, chilis, and fennel seeds. Season with salt and sauté over low heat for 10 minutes.

2. Dissolve the miso in 1/2 cup (125 ml) of boiling water. Stir the miso mixture and remaining water into the soup. Simmer until the potatoes are tender, 15-20 minutes. Add the watercress, snow peas, and lemon juice. Simmer for 3 minutes more. Garnish with the extra watercress and serve hot.

POTATO & WAKAME miso soup

Serves 6-8 • Preparation 10 minutes • Cooking 10-15 minutes Difficulty 1

2	tablespoons instant dashi stock granules		potatoes, peeled and cut into small cubes
6	cups (1.5 liters) boiling water	5	tablespoons (75 ml) white miso paste
14	ounces (400 g)	2	teaspoons wakame

1. Put the dashi stock granules in a saucepan with the boiling water and stir well.

2. Add the potatoes to the pan. Simmer until almost tender, 8-10 minutes (depending on the size of the cubes).

3. Place the miso paste in a small bowl and add a ladleful of the hot stock, whisking well to get rid of any lumps. When smooth, slowly pour the mixture back into the saucepan, whisking constantly.

4. Add the wakame and simmer for 1-2 minutes. Serve hot in small soup bowls.

ENOKI MUSHROOM & SCALLION miso soup

2	tablespoons instant dashi stock granules
6	cups (1.5 liters) boiling water
4	ounces (120 g) enoki mushrooms
2	tablespoons (30 ml) red miso paste
3	tablespoons (45 ml) white miso paste
4	ounces (120 g) silken tofu, cut into small cubes
2	scallions (spring onions), trimmed and thinly sliced on the diagonal

Serves 6–8 • Preparation 10 minutes • Cooking 8–10 minutes
Difficulty 1

1. Dissolve the dashi stock in the boiling water in a saucepan, stirring well. Add the enoki mushrooms.

2. Place both types of miso paste in a small bowl and add a ladleful of the hot dashi stock, whisking to get rid of any lumps. When the mixture is smooth, slowly pour it back into the saucepan, whisking constantly. Add the tofu and return to a simmer. Add the scallions and simmer for 1–2 minutes.

3. Ladle the soup evenly into six to eight small soup bowls and serve hot.

ASPARAGUS & TOFU miso soup

2   tablespoons instant dashi
     stock granules
6   cups (1.5 liters) boiling water
12   asparagus spears
5   tablespoons (75 ml) white
     miso paste
2   tablespoons mirin
2   tablespoons soy sauce
12   ounces (350 g) silken tofu, cut
     into small cubes

Serves 6–8 • Preparation 10 minutes • Cooking 8–10 minutes
Difficulty 1

1. Dissolve the dashi stock in the boiling water in a saucepan, stirring well. Add the asparagus to the pan. Simmer for 3 minutes over medium heat.

2. Place the miso paste in a small bowl and add a ladleful of the hot dashi stock, whisking to get rid of any lumps. When the mixture is smooth, slowly pour it back into the saucepan, whisking constantly. Add the mirin, soy sauce, and tofu. Heat through gently, without boiling.

3. Ladle the soup evenly into six to eight small soup bowls and serve hot.

INDEX